History of the Celts

by Clayton N. Donoghue

Produced by:

FriesenPress
Suite 300 – 852 Fort Street
Victoria, BC, Canada V8W 1H8

www.friesenpress.com

Distributed to the trade by The Ingram Book Company

Table of Contents

List of Illustrations

Tristan Logo, Ireland fun facts (start of every chapter)

INTRODUCTION

*"The river Ister rises among the Celts and the town of
Pyrene and crosses the whole of Europe. The Celts
Are beyond the Pillars of Hercules, next to the
Cynette, who live further west of all the peoples of Europe."*

HERODIUS

ot another book on the Celts! You would think
there is now enough of them around; what more can be
said about the subject? Well that's a good question, and
the answer is, there is a lot more that can be said of the
Celts. After all they were around for a lot longer than our
modern society and as such technically the literature on
them should be in greater volume then everything that
has happen in the last say 300-600 years. However, as we
know this is not the case and therefore it is hoped in this
small book I can bring out some new points that have not
been written previously.

From everything I have read, it is understandable that people would think everything there is to know about the Celts has already been written. The problem is that what I have found especially in the academic world is they go over the same material time and time again only adding some personal tidbit and calling it a day. What seems to be missing is the insight into what they are writing. For example Celtic swords have been found across Europe in the thousands, whereas Roman swords are the complete opposite. They are very rare and what few exist are in very poor condition. Now, if the Romans were this almighty, technologically advanced society their sword artifacts would reflect it; apparently not. Their metallurgy skills, turns-out, were not quite as advanced as the Celts'. Even in Julius Caesar's writings he openly admits it. Now why is that? If all there is to know about the Celts is known why is this small simple point not revealed in just about any book written about them so far? The answer is that historians for the most part simply address as quickly as they can an overall picture of the people and leave it at that. Thus we continuously hear when the Celts were first started, the language they spoke, the mythical legends they created, and when the glorious Romans crushed them. The end!

This book is deliberately kept small so you can quickly get to see some of the points that greater authors have missed in their enormous academic analogies. Speaking of which, have you ever sat down to seriously read a university book on this subject or for that matter any subject? They all seem to fit the same pattern. First they are extremely hard to read because of the high-end words that are continuously used; you almost think they're written in a foreign language. Second, you find the writer really does not form his own opinion, he merely reflects all the other authors' works in his own. If his research was principally made up of negative references, ultimately his book has the same view. After having written an academic paper myself in engineering one of the things I discovered is that various reference sources which are commonly believed to be credible are not true at all. This leads into the last point on the academics which is that they follow the names rather than the research. As soon as a reference source has a doctorate title, it's automatically taken as gospel. Maybe in the subject of history you can be careless with the facts but in engineering you can't. Technology is changing all the time and what a professor may have been correct about a few years ago is likely no longer the case today.

One of the things I'm really amused by when it comes to the Celts is their "Indo European Identity." It seems to me whoever came up with this simplistic generalization ought to have his head examined. I have come to the conclusion that the authors who use this term are somewhat lazy writers. They can't be bothered to carefully look at the Celts more analytically and so simply write the whole subject off as "Indo European." It's like saying the Anglo Saxons are Danish in origin for after all it was in Denmark where they originated from. The truth is the English, as we know them today, came from three distinct races and they of course were the Angles, Jutes, and the Saxons. Each of these races contributes a specific aspect to the merged

culture we now call English. The same is true with the Celts, who are comprised of the Scythians, Germans, and Ionics. Of the three the Scythians are the only group that brings in the Indo-European element to the merged culture of Celts. To say the entire people are "Indo-European" is sheer nonsense. Archaeology of their artifacts clearly shows influences from the Etruscans, Greeks, Germans, and of course the Scythians. This is one of the many things I hope to bring to the reader's attention as you progress through the book.

Next we come to the time frame. I will go into great detail on this point. Somehow when you read the various books on the when the Celts came into existence and how long the civilization existed you definitely get a mixed bag of opinions. From what I have seen we again come into a fast methodology to sum it up quickly. The Hallsatt burial sites appear to have been the popular reference point for when the Celts first came into existence (500 BC) and for bizarre reasons everything principally ended with Julius Caesar c. 54 AD. Somehow the Celtic era in Britain under Roman occupation does not count as a continuation of the Celts on account of the fact that they no longer have any presence on the mainland of Europe. I personally find this nothing short of ridiculous. When you just take one comparative example of say World War Two, Germany was not declared defeated until their high command formally signed the surrender papers. Hitler had been dead for nearly a week and the country was completely destroyed, yet to officials that still did not matter. The high command had to sign the documents before it became legal. Yet when it comes to the Celts, academics don't allow them the same courtesy. Ireland is the most remarkable on this point for they were never taken by the Romans, and the Celtic culture went on right up to the when the Normans came in the 1100's. Here too I will be spending a fair bit of time. As such it will be found the Celtic civilization existed a lot longer than experts are prepared to admit. My conjecture on this is the Pro-Roman writers possibly don't like the idea the Celtic civilization lasted longer than the Roman Empire did. The Roman Empire basically only existed for a thousand years; however going from the pre-Hallstatt age to right up to when the Irish fell to the Normans the Celts survived in Europe in their pure form for well over two thousand years.

Next are the three major empires that evolved from the Celtic world. Sounds pretty incredible, for only now the subjects are finally coming to light which is still another point to show that not all is yet known of the Celts and this is a big one. The first empire that now a few authors have at last recognized is the Celtic Empire that was firmly in place by 277 BC. Sure it was not managed as we came to expect in Rome, but nonetheless it was an empire. At the peak of their existence the Celts occupied all of Europe for well over a hundred years. Their territory ranged from the Crimea down into northern Turkey as far west as Portugal and from central Italy all the way up to the northern tip of Scotland. The second empire was the Irish empire under King Niall of the Nine Hostages. Only in Ireland today and partially in Britain is this unique empire finally acknowledged. It is hard to believe from contemporary history of the country that this little Island of a nation was at one time on the verge of conquering Britain. Had Vortigern not called in the Saxons for help, who knows what Britain today may have turned out to be. Lastly there was the Celtic Church

Empire; this church which originated in Ireland swept virtually all of Britain and central Europe and lasted for well over 300 years.

It is on that note where I end my book. The reason for this is that is the last of the Celtic cultural influence in the whole of Europe basically ends there. Sure I could go on to write about the Scots, the Irish, the Amoricans, the Cornish, and the Welsh from after the Norman era, but it seems to me that would be dealing with independent states of nationalistic perspective rather than a truly Celtic continuation.

Chapter 1

The Beginning and the Hallstatt Celts

*"Their vanity therefore makes them unbearable in victory,
while defeat plunges them into the deepest despair
their thoughtlessness is also accompanied by traits of
barbarity and savagery, as is so often the case with the
population of the north." STRABO*

The beginning of the Celts was centred in Europe and like all cultures it went through several stages of development as it matured to what we know of them today. In this opening it's going to be learned what distinguished them from the very beginning and how, through their expansion across the continent, they actually absorbed traits that belonged to other nations. When you look carefully you will discover that the Celts are a mixture of many cultures that they themselves were able to impose their own identity on. Further there are many aspects of the Celts we claim today are Celtic when in fact they are anything but.

The earliest confirmation of the time when the Celts came into existence is around 800 BC. An archaeological find in Halstatt, Austria by Johann George Ramsauer circa 1855 was a defining moment. It was as a result of this discovery that the Celts in that period began to becalled the Hallstatt Celts. The pattern continued at La Tène Switzerland in another archaeological find of Celts that existed circa 350 BC and therefore became known as the as the La Tène period. The second period was claimed to be characterized by a major cultural evolution in the people. As a result the two periods were quite distinct.

The first mention of the Celts was in the classical world by a man name Herodotus. He referred to the race as "Keltoi," which means mysterious people. However, it is found that through others like Titus and Julius Caesar the name resurfaced many times throughout the ancient world. It is claimed the Celts did not call them themselves Celts, nor did they have a name to identify themselvesas certain kind of nation. The people operated on a tribal basis. They knew with each by their tribes that they were of a similar people; this is confirmed in the various wars they had with both the Greeks and the Romans. Brennus (I) who is one of the very first to launch a campaign against the Romans circa 387 BC gathered Celts from all over central Europe. This was again repeated with Vercingetorix in 55 BC in the Gaulic rebellion against Caesar. As mentioned the Celts referred to each other by the tribal nations they came from; for example you have the Belgae, the Iceni, the Dumonian, the Brigantes, and the Aduans, just to mention a few. It is like the North

American Indians; they did not have a name for the type of people they were. They too called themselves by their tribal identity, like the Cree, the Iroquois, the Wendets, the Ottawas, and the Black Foot.

It's been long discussed where the Celts evolved from. It seems to me that to avoid any strenuous research the various writers simply say they are evolved from Indo – Europeans. The question is who were the Indo-Europeans? The earliest sources I have found were the Scythians, Germans, and Ionians. The Scythians seemed to be the dominant group, like the Saxons were the dominant group of the Jute-Anglo-Saxon mix. The Scythians are our closest link to the Indo-Asian culture. It was claimed that the Persians and Etruscans played roles as well because of what has been found in the Celtic burials. However, this was later dismissed because of people like Strabo, confirmed some of the artifacts were the results of who the Celts traded with. In 800 BC the Celts had commerce largely with the Mediterranean nations. They had a particular liking for Greek and Etruscan wine. The Hochdorf burial, excavated by archaeologist Hans Hildebrant, just north of the Halsatt in southern Germany, was the cultural confirmation to this point. The Hochdorf grave was dated to 600 BC and with it they were able to define exactly what Celtic was and what was items from just common trade were. It turned out it was simple matter of comparing the two sites, Halstatt and Hochdorf, for their common art forms. As an example, the neck torc was one of the items that distinguished the Celtic people.

HOCHDORF BURIAL

The Hastatt period was thoroughly explored to see to what extent did it grow and where did it have its influences culturally speaking. The reason for this is because there seems to have developed a bit of confusion between them and another culture known as the Urnfield people, who existed long before the Celts ever came into existence. Their time frame is around 3,000 BC and was centred in what is now Portugal. They expanded east and north into Britain, Ireland, and central France. Many stone monuments, particularly Stonehenge and New Grange, are from this culture and not the Celts'. Yet you will still find people in the tourist industry that will say otherwise. Another group from the Urnfield people's era was the Druids. To this day they are associated with the Celts but it appears this isn't true at all. The Druids, when you take the time to study them, did have a lot to do with the great stone monuments. Thus it seems they were originally from the Urnfield people and not the

Celts. The Druids will be addressed in more detail later on. Lastly the Urnfield people lived in rectangular houses and were principally an agricultural society as compared the nomadic existence of the Celts.

So how did the various aspects of the Urnfield people get mixed in with the Celts? It seems the answer lies in the fact that the Celts were a warring, conquering people, and the truth centres in their migration. In it, they took on various cultural aspects of the people they conquered, many of whom were the builders of the stone monuments, as well as the Druids. Strabo and Julius Caesar were two sources of the migrating nature of the Celts. It seemed that once the Celts grew into a tribal "nation" they naturally started to expand their territory.

When you look into the Scythian influence on the Celts they were for the most part nomadic. The Celts were not ones to sit around. It was learned that horsemanship was a major part of the Celts' identity. As such it stands to reason why they were always on the go. The Scythians are said to have come from the Russians Steppes. There seems to be a pattern of behaviour that whatever culture evolved from the Steppes, like the Huns, Cossacks, and Scythians, were all great horsemen.

It is from their origins that the reputation of being warlike people was earned. When you mix in the German element there also develops a powerful determination as well. When you read up on Titus' writings of the Germans, you discover the physical strength of the Celtic people. When the first Celtic slaves were brought to Rome by Cecio, their physical appearance was said to evoke nothing short of envy. The Celts were described as muscular, tall and blond; this was said of their women as well. To the dark haired short Romans these slaves inspired wonder and likely went for a great price as well.

This naturally begs the question: which of the claimed three cultures had the most influence on the Celtic race It seems to be a bit of a tossup on this point. In appearance, the Germans seem to have won out. Celts are described as being unusually big with blonde hair. However, when it came to the horsemanship and Chariots, the Scythians win out. And when we go into the structural and engineering developments, the Ionian or Mediterranean culture side of the people is dominant. When you see the craftsmanship of the Celts you can see they were a lot more sophisticated people than they are given credit for.

When you examine the Hochdorf grave along with the grave of the Vix burial near Burgundy France, you come across some amazing artifacts. The Vix burial is also dated 480 BC, and is thatof a Celtic Princess. Her burial was just as elaborate as that at the Hochdorf site. In her grave was found a beautifully designed bronze vase. The motifs on it are claimed to be clearly Celtic and no other influence. Mind you there is a small controversy around her burial on account that she was buried on a chariot and that is typical of La Tène culture. However, she was fully identified as a princess; therefore, many scholars place her still in the Hallstatt era. So it would seem that the burial of the Princess of Vix may have happened during transitional period as the Celts went from the Hallstatt to the La Tène period.

The vase becomes a common feature of the Celts in a later period. It turns out when it comes to bronze workmanship and tin-smithing the Celts were the very best in all of Europe at the time. The skill of tin making came from trade with the Etruscans and the Ligurians in the Alps. In Caesar's writings, the Romans were not particularly in favour of invading the Celts especially in Britain because it was felt that it would have an impact on the tin trade. The Celts had a reputation for making the best mirrors in the known world at that time. Caesar in his writings clearly states needed a pretext for the invasion of Gaul; otherwise the senate would never allow it.

To what extent did the Halstatt period expand to? In terms of the time frame it seems it is confirmed that the period was from around 800 BC to 350 BC. During that time the culture spread into Western Europe as far as Portugal and Ireland. The Urnfield people were completely absorbed into the Celtic race. It is through the language as well as art that modern archaeologists are able to fully determine the Hallstatt era. It is found to be certain now that the Irish and Scots are the source from which came the surviving elements of this time period.

The concentration of the Hallstatt was primarily in Austria and up along the Rhine. From here they move east slightly into Germany, but principally moved west. This becomes a special point to note when we start to look at the La Tène; the migration now begins to move east and south. The farthest extent of the La Tène period is into Turkey with a people known as the Galatians and into the Po Valley of Italy. However, The La Tène culture also migrates west as well but never makes it into Ireland, Scotland or Portugal. As such there is a lot of overlapping of the two time periods and it comes as no surprise that there was lot of confusion in the process.

Map of the Hallstatt (west) and La Tène (east) regions

The burials of the Hallsatt were first the distinguishing mark of the Celts compared with that of the Urnfield culture; it would later differentiate them from the La Tène Celts. The Urnfield people cremated cremated their dead while the Hallstatt Celts buried their dead in the typical manner of the Mediterranean world. It was found once the Celts absorbed the Urnfield people they stayed with the practice of their type of burial, but they did develop a cremation practice for their enemies. The wicker man-style execution is claimed to have been a common practice amongst the Celts. Bodies were thrown into a huge wicker figure of a man and then set on fire.

In terms of the distinctions between the Hallstatt and the La Tène, they centered on the carts they buried with the bodies. In the Hallstatt period the body was accompanied by a wagon. In the La Tène period the body was placed on a chariot and then buried. The Hochdorf and Vix burials are examples of the Hallstatt era's. However, in a burial of Somme-Bionne near the Marne France, the person is buried on a chariot. This is where the dividing line is made between the two eras. It is also from these three burials that they were able to distinguish the cultural evolution of the people themselves. In the Hochdorf burial it is clearly recognized the society was a chiefdom. However, in the Somme-Bionne burial this was an elite warrior who was buried. From this point on we see there is a common pattern with all the La Tène sites, in that nearly all were warriors being buried and no longer just Kings and Queens. This probably explains the change in the temperament in the classical world when it came to the Celts.

The Hallstatt period was rooted in trade and their main export at the time was salt. As mentioned the Celts were also exporting metals such as tin and bronze. All the indications show the Celts naturally developed into a very sophisticated nation. Their style of art became well-established in this time period. According to the Greek writers at the time there was no evidence of the Celts being a hostile people with any of the Mediterraneans. It does seem contradictory that they rapidly expanded to the west against a people that were culturally farther advanced themselves, yet made no similar expansions east or south. One can only guess the Celts perhaps knew the limits of their military prowess.

From all indications the Hallstatt period peaked around 400 BC. The burials found from 480 to 400 BC are said to all to be very elaborate. Clearly the Celtic economy was at its highest point then. The Mediterranean influences in the Celtic world have also peaked in this time as well. After this the Greek and Etruscan artifacts in the burial sites start to disappear. You can see the Celts were evolving into a new age.

Expansion and the La Tène Celts

La Tène is in west Switzerland and it is claimed this is where the new major cultural development of the Celts happened. It is said that it is here where the most archaeological evidence of the new Celtic era is found. La Tène marked a significant cultural period, not so much as a political change; mind you there is plenty of proof of this observation as well. The style of art became more decorative and it is said the Book of Kells is the best representation of it. Also, the engineering of the Celts seems to have been refined in this era. For example the metallurgy in their weapons was said to be the very best in all of Europe. They developed chain mail and seamless steel rim wheels in their chariots. Also, they came up with their own alcohol known as 'mead.' Up until this point the Celts had largely imported wine from the Etruscans.

The La Tène period is dated around 350 BC. Politically and socially the Celts had evolved from a chiefdom-style society to a warrior based society. When we start to read great legends like the Tan Bo (Ireland) we get an idea on how it worked. Leaders for example were no longer naturally brought to the throne based on royal lineage, they were now elected. In order to win that election you had to prove yourself as a great warrior. Also, it did not mean you were elected in for life. You held office only as long as you could continue to prove yourself as a great warrior. The moment you could no longer sustain yourself as a fearless and wise leader you were voted out of office as was the case with Vortigern of Britain c. 460 AD, or as was often the case, the Druids had you ceremonially executed. Evidence of this can be found in the various museums in Denmark and Great Britain.

Apparently one of our first written records of the social change that came from the La Tène era was by a Roman writer: Polybius, c. 200 BC. He writes there was a massive population explosion amongst the Celts in central Gaul. A Celtic leader by the name of Ambigatus took with him about five major Celtic nations and migrated into what is now Hungary. The size of the nation was said to be well over 400,000. From here one of his nephews took a portion of that group and migrated into the Italian Alps (Milan). This is said to all have taken place around 300 BC. According to yet another Roman writer, Trogus, there was another major migration from central Gaul and with a population of 300,000 they too settled in Hungary. So suddenly you have this huge new population of Celts just on the doorstep of the Greeks.

Like any emerging nation they started to draw notice by others and for the first time the Celts were being carefully examined. At this time a Greek historian, Diodorus Siculuss, wrote about the Celts, their appearance and behaviour. As mentioned the Celts had evolved from a chiefdom-like-society to a distinct warrior base. They are described as clean shaven except for their enormous mustaches. Their clothing was brightly checkered and striped and with their now trademark identity of torcs around their necks. Also, they wore beautifully designed brooches, often of made from gold, silver, or iron. They were very proud of their physical appearances; both men and women are said to be tall and very muscular. A lot of the time appearing nude was not uncommon, especially in battle. For the most part in battle they had their blond hair washed in lime and shaped into long spikes to have a more fearsome appearance. In their personal nature they were described as boastful people, singing bards and quick to merry making with lots of drink. Feasting was a favourite passtime. However, in these feasts fighting broke out, often with fatal results.

The first Celtic hill fort is said to have been built near Stuttgaard, Germany. It was named Heuneberg Hill Fort and was dated 530 BC. Up until now the Celts did have fortifications built that were generally viewed as more reinforced towns and villages. Again, we have to remember the Celts were by and large nomadic in nature. When we actually start to examine the Celtic homes we see they was very temporary structures. However, in the

Heunberg Hill Fort we have another sign of the changing nature of the Celtic society. In this fort was found the remains of a metal smith operation. A variety of different types of metal were uncovered, so it was deemed that the Celts were now mastering their own metallurgy skills. It came to be realized later by the Romans, especially their military that Celtic swords were made of a higher degree of craftsmanship then their own.

When we go to Britain there may be some confusion on the subject of forts considering it has been well established that the famous Maiden Fortress in southern England was built around 1000 BC. However, once again it has to be remembered these forts and many like it across the United Kingdom were built by their predecessors: the Urnfield people. The Celts simply occupied them and did some new alterations to them. Mind you the Celts, as time went on, did start to build their own style forts too.

Celtic forts, like their jewelry and political structures, had a profound change from the Halstatt period to the La Tène period. It is believed that the Urnfield people were the influential force at this point. Prior to 400 BC, Celtic forts were rectangular in shape and after they started taking a more oval design. More of this will be discussed later when addressing who the Celts were as a society.

Celtic Forts

Because the Celts were a mobile people, their forts were not designed very elaborately like the Romans'. In the Hallstatt age there were a number of forts found in Germany that followed the typical rectangular

Mediterranean method. However, not too many were built. Again we go back to the tuathe kingdom basic principle of the Celts. They did not have large population centers. They were a rural society.

Evidence shows that as the Celts migrated west into the Urnfield people's territory they took on their style of fort building, plus added a few of their own features. A Celtic fortress was a wooden palisade circular in shape. Most were small and seem to have an average area in space of not more than 4,200 square feet. Again this reflects their tribal mentality. It comes as no surprise that it was very easy for the Romans, and later the Normans, to burn them down with the use of archers or catapults. The reason for the type of design is for the Celts' weaponry consisted of spears, swords, and shields. They did not have archers in their military. Well distinguished forts that are said to be clearly Celtic are, Gergovia (Gaul), Aleacia (Gaul), Dunadd (Dal Riada), Tara (Hybernia) and cashel (Hybernia). Fort Maiden in Wessex is dated as far back as 2000 BC so it's likely was an Urn field fortress that was later occupied from the migration of the Celts to Britain.

The larger forts like Tara and Dunadd were the national seats. As such there are not many of them around. These fortresses again were in a manner of speaking pretty small, for archeologist have established they could not hold more than 700 or so people in them. When you consider a single Roman legion comprised of 5,000 men even the largest of Celtic forts were no match to hold out against Roman attacks.

The last little feature that should be mentioned in a typical Celt fort is the base. They are recognizable of the spiral effect that rises gently to be ultimately crowned by the fort itself. For the most part it was simple earth built up but also as was found in Dundurn Fortress of Strathclide Celtic Forts being made from a pile up of rocks. The rocks were held in place with a lace like effect with logs, and even on a side of a cliff the design was such that it would still hold.

Next, before we start to get into the actual conflicts the Celts had with their Mediterranean neighbors I will just one more time explain the La Tène migration through Europe. Like the Hallstatt period there was a natural migration of the new age yet again. As before the Celts migrated as far as Spain which at the time was known by the Romans as Iberia, it is believed they pushed out the Hallstatt Celts who are said to have migrated in a "second invasion" of Ireland. The La Tène Celts migrated as far north as Denmark. In their nation museum in Copenhagen are some really incredible examples of the influence the new age had on the Celts already present. Then of course was mentioned the Celts migrating to what is now Hungary and Italy's Po valley. Scholars generally agree the migration period happened between 350 AD to roughly 280 BC. In this time frame there were numerous examples of violent takeovers; however by and large it is recognized that it for the most part as peaceful. This does seem very strange when to this point in time the Celts are now more war-like then ever before. Once we get into the actual conflict you will better understand the differences.

CHAPTER 2

The Celtic language

It would seem that the in the most fundamental terms, the Celts spoke Gaelic. However, like all cultures there were a variety of different dialects. Also, it comes as no surprise their language, like all languages, evolved over time. Here we are going to take a glimpse into the Gaelic identity and its evolution. There are two principal forms of the language that originated from the two major cultural periods of Halstatt and La Tène. The first one is known as Goedilic and the second one is known as Brethonic. Examples will be provided so you can see the distinction between them. Lastly it comes as no surprise these fundamentals break down even further with modern nation development such as the Welsh, Scottish, Irish, and Cornish, just mention a few.

The year is 387 BC and Brennus (I), with a force of 250,000 men, is on the march to Rome. He has probably the largest Celtic army known in history. The most fundamental question from this huge operation is how did he communicate with the other Celts when it's generally believed they all came from tribal like nations across Europe? When you follow Julius Caesar's letters you get the distinct impression the Celts were just a series of tribes with little in common with each other, only that they were made up a similar type race and nothing more. Well when we look at Brennus's enormous army we find this isn't true at all. The fundamental similarity between all the assorted Celtic nations that were present was their common Gaelic language.

Scholars as I have seen have gone into great debate over the last 200 years as the true authenticity of the language. However, it seems just like Brennus's army a common thread does appear in all the different discussions on it.

The language the Celts spoke in its most primary identification is called Celtic. Upon further study into the language and its people the name gets a more refined recognition and that is Gaelic. By the best consensus, the language origins are said to be Indo-European. Again, this is a term that many can't exactly pin down to what it means. As such depending upon who you want to take reference from the language seems to have a wide variety of different specific influences. Apparently, it is claimed there is Teutonic, Slavic, Greek, German, and even Latin all mixed in together. And just to make things even more interesting it is felt there are various words that camefrom India.

With that type of opening you wonder how is even possible to make any sense of the language. Well you are not alone if you have come to this type of conclusion. Ask David Ellis Evans of Britain; when he did his exhaustive study of the language he concluded Gaelic is the most frustrating language known and does not support any observation that the language has a connection to any other culture. Yet the irony here is that this position is not conclusive when the scholarly world generally agrees that the Celts were in fact derived from three principle nations, Scythian, German, and Ionian. It seems obvious that if this is the case then Gaelic must be a fundamental mix of these three.

The first dissecting of the language, as with so many others, is to find some common words. In this case they found one word in Gaelic that had a similar pronunciation to those in two other languages and as such were able to find the beginning of a base. The word was "King." In Sanskit the word is "Raj". In Latin the word is pronounced "Rex." And, in Gaelic the word is "Ri." The person who made the discovery of this common connection was Colin Renfrew in 1973. Renfrew was an archaeologist, and he further concluded that the words that have no association to any known language must have come from the Urnfield culture. There is merit to this observation for it is accepted that the Celts in their migration did absorbed many of the customs of the people they took over, and the language would not be excluded.

On this point we come across J.P. Mallory, who goes even further to say the Celtic language is all Proto-Celtic. Proto-Celtic is claimed to have been the language spoken by the Urnfield people. With the recent development in the study of the Celts a new line of thinking is emerging on this very topic. It is now coming to believe the

Urnfield people were "pre-Celts." If this comes to be an established point it will definitely change everything that has been written up to this time.

Now before I go any further, I have to reiterate that the Celts did not have a written language like the Romans and Greeks. All the study on the Gaelic language is simply based on what has survived to today. It is said it was not until 1700 when the various forms of the Gaelic language, like Irish, Scottish, and Welsh was first put down in writing. This becomes a crucial point to keep in mind as we see how other people have come to define the language.

The two great cultural movement of the Celts that are certain were the Hallstatt period, time frame, 800-400 BC; and the La Tène period, time frame 350 BC – 450 AD. There is more than enough archaeological evidence to support this claim to being true. We know physically where the two migration journey across Europe and where they more importantly stopped. This becomes another point to note when we discover there are two fundamental forms of the Gaelic language. From the Hallstatt age the Gaelic language is referred to as the Goedilic dialect. It

would appear that when the La Tène age came to prominence the language had a major evolutionary change and from it the Gaelic language now had what is called the Brethonic dialect.

How these two distinctions came about was the examinations of the contemporary Celtic cultures of in around the United Kingdom. It was found that Wales, Cornwall, and Breton all spoke a similar type of Gaelic. Ireland, Scotland, and the Island of Man spoke yet another similar version of Gaelic as well. It's when you go to archaeology you are able to know the sources of the two versions. The Hallstatt Celts actually made it across the whole of the British islands. The La Tène Celts only made it to Wales and Northumbria In the lowlands of Scotland you experience the most unique example where the two versions coexist. In one village they will speak Brethonic Gaelic and in the very next they'll speak Goedilic Gaelic. From this is the confirmation the borderline of the two cultures meeting.

The distinction between the two dialects can be heard; Goedilic sounds very hard and the other, Brethonic, sounds very soft in its word pronunciations. In the 1700s when the two versions were now in the written format another discovery was made where came yet another simpler identification of the languages. Note the following examples of modern Irish and Welsh:

Word	Irish (hard C)	Welsh (Soft P)
HEAD	CEANN	PEN
WHO	CE'	PWY
FOUR	CEATHER	PEDWAR
SON OF,	MAC	AP

From this analysis the two versions were now addressed as 'Brethonic "P"' – Gaelic and 'Goedilic "Q"' – Gaelic. These terms later popularized the phrase, *"Mind your P's and Q's."* . The person who did the research into this was Edward Lhayd. The study that fully confirmed that Brethonic and Goedilic were authentic versions of the Gaelic was done in 1882 by Sir John Rhys. What makes this important to know is now where the modern versions of Gaelic like Irish and Welsh come from.

Looking at a map of the Roman Empire at the time, we find there are several distinct regions of Celts there. In the now France was Gaul. The Romans referred to that type of Celt as Gaulish. In the now Spain region was Iberia. The Romans called that Celtic as KeltoiIberian. Further there was the Lusitanian Celtic language. In Briton (Britain) the language was identified as Britonic. Finally in the Swiss Alps the Celtic language there was identified as Lepontic. I have not seen any actual documents such as Caesar's letters to support these identifications. I am only going by the various academic references who claim this was the case. As many will know, the Romans were very dismissive of the Celts as simply being barbarians and undeserving of any recognition of their language whatsoever. The reason the Romans did not know the various Gaelic languages is because they all sounded basically all the same.

On that point there is an interesting subscript to this in that in 1983 a discovery was made from an archaeological dig at Larzac near Averyron. Here was found a tablet of about a 160 words by a Roman tradesman of what is described as the actual Celtic language of the time. It is felt this is the only known source they now have to the Gaulish language. Unfortunately, they have yet to actually study it to know for certain the type of Gaelic it actually is.

Finally we now come to where the sources are from the now fully recognizable bases of the modern versions of Gaelic still spoken today. Scottish and Irish were easily recognized and are from Goedilic. Cornish and Welsh are also easily recognizable, and traceble to Brethonic. What became a bit of a brief mystery was the Amorican Gaelic spoken in Breton France. This version of Gaelic is also Brethonic. How this occurred was that in the 5th century Britons who were escaping from the Saxons migrated to Breton and brought with them the Brythonic version of the language.

As far as research shows the Gaulish, Lepontic, and Celtoiberian languages are extinct, due to centuries of Roman occupation. The Pictish language of Scotland is also claimed extinct. This was due to Irish conquest of the country circa 400 AD.

So now we go back to Brennus and his massive military force that did indeed sack the city of Rome. The common language everyone spoke in his army was Brethonic Gaelic.

Chapter 3

Crannogs and Chariots

Round my throne
Three fiery rings,
In my courtyard
fountain spring

ARIANHOOD

I chose to give this chapter a little more exciting title than simply saying 'Homes of the Celts,' though that is what it is about. It seems to me by understanding the Celts' home life and their ingenuity you learn they were indeed a lot more advanced than they are given credit for. The Celts had superior standards in equipment than the Romans did, unfortunately because of their political structure they could not implement them with the same degree of efficiency.

A *crannog* is for the most part described as a circular wooden structure on stilts in a body of water. However, on various occasions it is also been found to mean a small village of Celtic homes. As was mentioned earlier the Celts did not live in large fortresses as the Romans did. What may have been seen as a fortress was better recognized as an over-sized community. The Celts had fortresses, but they were separated from the community centres such as the famed Alesia.

The crannog was typical of how the nuclear Celts lived. This was a small single walled palisade community of maybe three of four homes. Likely the family, their slaves, and their animals all dwelled together. Why there was a wall was to protect them from wild animals, not attacks from other communities. It is hard to visualize today when much of Europe is an open field but 2000 years ago it was principally made up of dense forest with wolves, bears, boars, and deer. When you read up on the Celtic legends hunting wildlife seemed to be common at the time. This environment was very conducive to the Celtic mentality. Their home life structure was, similarly, of a temporary nature as well. In the 350 BC period there was a lot of migration going on and it was only possible because the Celts were able to uproot and move. Rebuilding a whole community was very easy to do.

The actual homes were remarkable little pieces of architectural design. If you have ever seen a picture of a Celtic house, it looks very simple in its round shape. Yet when you examine it closely you quickly grasp the Celts were quite clever in the building of it. The Celts realized something in the very foundations that even campers today still often forget when they put up a tent, and that is if it rains for anything length of time the water will leak underneath the walls. Thus when a structure was to be started the first thing that happened was a circular hole was dug at about 3 feet. It was then filled with stone sticks and branches in a very haphazard many. Then was is covered over with a layer of soil. As you can readily tell the foundation was porous in nature. If it rained the runoff wouldseep into the ground and keep the interior dry.

The next step was building a circular wicker fence about 4 feet high and another one on the inside same height. From what I have seen the standard diameter on the inside was an average of 30 feet. The distance between the two fence walls was around 2 feet. There was a marked seal cut off for a doorway to the structure. Once that was done sand and earth was now filled in between the two walls, up to the top of the two walls. Y now had a solid frame for the roof to be build on top of.

From here a long pole was placed in the centre of the interior circle, and lashed to its top several long branches that extended onto the wall in a full 360 degree fashion. At about a foot or so above the wall were lashed cross braces to the long ribs. However, this was only done to every other set, for more ribs would be attached and then were lashed with crass braces as well. Eventually this would make a roof frame that came to a point, the cross braces getting smaller as they reached the top.

If you've ever been to Ireland, the Irish cottage roof with its hay cover is still to this day done in the original manner of that of the Celts. The hay is grabbed into small hand size bundles and tied off at one end. The length is the distance between the cross braces of the roof frame. The hand bundle is then divided in half making a "V" shape. From here it is slid over the brace and the extended portion lies on top of the brace below. This is repeated at the base until there is a complete fill around the top of the wall. Then you go up to the next level and do the same. Gradually you make it near to the top and a hay roof is constructed. At the top, the hay bundled is now deliberately thinned out. The reason for this is so the interior smoke can escape, and to provide protection to keep the rain out.

The centre pole is then removed and the walls are lime-covered past for sealing purposes. Presto, you have a Celtic home. As can be seen this structure is not of a permanent design; so taking it apart because of natural wood rot is very easy to do for the purpose of rebuilding.

The interior is furnished primarily with assorted animal skins and wicker mats of straw. Wolf skin is said was the preferred because of the warm, soft nature of the animal hair. In the centre of the circular pattern were the camp fire and an iron pot fixed on a tri-stick frame over it. The Celts did not have chairs, but did make low level table to place their meals and drinks on them. At the time of the Norman invasion of Ireland in the 10th century drawing were made of the Irish Celt festivals and you can see how the natives sat on the ground and ate off the small tables.

Typical Celtic Dwelling picture

Now if you can visualize several of these small crannogs stretching across an area, the next level of community is now known as a *tuathe,* or in Scottish terminology
a clan. All the regionalized crannogs are of a similar
family name are headed by a clan chief. Again, it is
not by birth hierarchy system as was the case with the
Saxons. The Chiefdom was elected to office by a vote of
the community. From here when you get into a series of
tuathes the next level is the province or provincial state.
In Julius Caesar's campaign letters you can see how he
names these various provincial/nation peoples of the
Gaul Territory. You have the Atrebates, Iceni, Averni,
Belgae, and Dumoni just to mention a few of the Celtic
tribal nations.

Getting back to the crannog, as was eluded to in the very beginning, it was an almost complete mini community at the family level. Livestock was for the most part the currency of exchange. Family wealth was determined by the number of cows, sheep, and pigs they had. When you start to address the Celtic Brehon law you can see that if a person is found guilty of an offence, payment was always measured out in terms of animal stock.

Farming has been found principally on the main continent of Europe with the Celts there and in the Vercingetorix rebellion of 46 BC crops are mentioned numerous times being destroyed to prevent it from falling into Roman hands. However, it is not until into the 3rd century it takes hold in Britain and Ireland. Archaeologist say the population growth dramatically increased once the skills of farming were mastered on the British Islands.

Everyday Life

I figure at this point taking a look at everyday life of the Celts may be necessary to get a better insight into what they were really like as compared to what numerous writers claim they were based on how they generally were seem by foreigners, particularly the Greeks and Romans. This is something Titus did with the Germans, and here too we find the people are a lot more admirable than the simple barbarians the Romans in general cast them to be. Perhaps the same can be developed with the Celts as well.

From the opening we have found the Celts were a nomadic mix of Germans, Scythians, and Greek Ionians or even Persians for that matter. Now there was a major cultural change in the people circa 350 BC. If they were war like before they were even more so now. In appearance they were a very muscular looking people; so it has to be assumed they lived a physical type life style. When you read the Tan Bo legends of Ireland you get your first confirmation to the La Tène influence over the everyday mentality of the people. The system, no longer Chiefdom oriented, meant everyone now had an opportunity to excel to greatness. This means when in the off seasons of war it is very likely the everyday Celt practiced is combat skills so one day he could be recognized as a warrior.

Through that lens, the so called quiet-looking crannog suddenly looks like a miniature training camp. Later we will be looking at the tools and weapons of the Celts in detail and it will show that the swords in particular were the finest ever made in the Iron Age. The King Arthur legends are yet another added confirmation of just how much the Celts treasured their swords.

As Julius Caesar himself told in his numerous letters, the Celts were not a uniform nation and as such did not have a standing army. The Celts were indeed a massive annual militia force, they fought in the good weather and returned homed in the fall to harvest and tend to their domiciles. Though it is only a fictional story I have found Steven Lawhead's *Arthur in his Pendragon* series to be one of the best examples of the reality of Celtic life. There is one chapter in the book when King Arthur is aware that the enemy army will be forced to leave the battle because it is getting to close to harvest. For him to get the advantage at this stage of his campaign he has a portion of his army to go and loot the enemy's harvest thus bringing what was generally viewed as an unorthodox victory. The enemy realized if they did not surrender they would starve that winter.

So with the intros out of the way let's take a look at the crannog and how it operated. As mentioned, the appearance is like a small garrison. There is the master family dwelling, one likely for storage of food and wine, another for their livestock and a third to house their slaves. From stories of Finn McCool, Nial of the Nine Hostages ,and Saint Patrick you learn readily the Celts did have slaves. In Ireland in the late 5th century slavery was a huge part of the economy. For obvious reasons the crannogs were located near a water source be it a river or stream for water supply. Next it was ideal to have the crannog in a forest for two reasons; one for a fuel source and the other for access to wild game. Greek writers have written more than enough on this subject; the Celts had a particular passion for fresh game meals like boar, deer, and the odd occasion bear. Excavations done in Emen Macha, Northern Ireland, found remains of bones from bears, so it not hard to assume that at some point in time the people of that community feasted on bears. Lastly, if the crannog was on the main continent there would be an open field of harvest.

Considering cauldrons have been excavated in their hundreds and the mention of them in Celtic folklore is frequent, it stands to reason that porridge and stews were probably the mainstay of their everyday diet. The best source I have found on this topic is again the legends of Finn McCool and the Welsh legends around the Taliesin. From these legends you get the impression the Celts had stews where fish was the main source of protein in the meal. As for drink, it beyond a proven point Etruscan wine was the most favoured beverage with the Hallstatt Celts. Later in around the 3rd century do we start to see the Celts have developed their own beverage known as mead, which is a very heavy, beer-like drink. It is claimed "ebulum" ale of Scotland is the closest surviving example of the ale the Celts brewed. You can to this day buy the brand as a novelty in that country.

Archaeologists have proven from the excavations of the late Hallstatt Age (circa 400 BC) the overall Celtic economy was thriving. In the national museum of Copenhagen you can see the extent of their wealth as Celts even had time for fashion. I was amazed to see that young girls sported woolen miniskirts and halter tops. In a barbaric age fashion like this does not even begin to reach our imagination, yet it happened. Found in every Celtic home were looms, combs, tin mirrors, jewelry, brooches, knives, wooden plates, urns, chains, leather, and of course the famous plaid woolen blankets. Gold was well distributed amongst the common public as well. It is said that Caesar had wagons-full when he ended his eight year campaign in Gaul.

The average life expectancy of a Celt was said to be not more than 30 years. Though it appeared the average Celt did have a fairly comfortable environment in which to live, their everyday behaviour seemed to dictate a much shorter life. A warrior-base community tends to experience to a lot of violence and the Greek writers have pointed this out on numerous occasions when addressing the Celtic society; especially at feast gatherings, Celtic warriors were seen getting up boasting of their greatness, when someone would challenge them and a bloody fight would soon result in a fatal conclusion. In this type of everyday living it is not conceivable the Celts could have survived long, even without the added problems of general diseases and the invading Romans. The Celts' secret to survival was procreation. In the letters of Saint Paul to the Galatians, the Celts were very open on this subject. Men did not confine their affection for their mates to the bedroom. To the emerging Christian world it probably appeared the most vulgar aspect of the Celts. Yet when you look at the way they lived the only thing they had going for them to prevent extinction was their sexual nature.

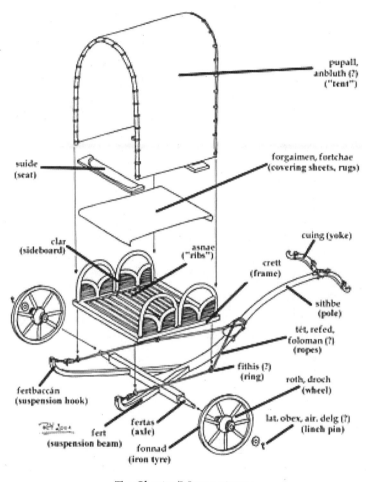

The Chariot/Wagon picture

Apparently the Romans did see Celtic chariots when they were in Gaul, but it would seem that their biggest experience with the weapon was in Britain. The Rebellion with Boudicca of the Iceni (c. 54 AD) showed the extent of damage the warriors could do to an enemy. How they were deployed was to they lead the attack with the infantry close behind them. For the defender it looked like the chariot was going to crash into them and if they did not have the nerve to hold their ground they would break ranks, which was the Celts' idea. The moment the enemy folded the Infantry following would rush through and with their long hacking swords would make quick work of the fleeing forces. However, the Celts found that the Romans held their formation, so the best that the charioteer could do was fly around in front; the warrior with him threw his spear and then would get out of the way of the main attack. Often it ended badly for the Celts who found they slammed into a wall of shields and could not swing their deadly swords. The Romans who had much shorter swords simply jabbed between the slits of the wall and cut down the Celts like a scythe to wheat.

At first glance at a Celtic Chariot you wonder how the two riders, driver, and warrior even stayed on the device when it was in full motion. It appears it was nothing more than a flat board on a single axel with an arm that extended out to the two horses that drove it. With a mechanism of this construction you might assume that with the first rock or fallen tree in a field both people on the vehicle would be immediately thrown off. However upon closer examination you quickly see the Celts were very much aware of this; it turns out the flat surface actually rested on two long ropes just above the axel. As it was there was suspension to absorb the shock of the vehicle when racing across the field. Thus we get our first glance at the truly amazing quality of Celtic engineering.

In one of the earliest contacts with the Celts the Romans also discovered with the chariot and later their wagons the seamless steel rims on them. The Romans found this to be pretty incredible for with their vehicles the wheels had a long flat bar folded around the rim and where they met nailed into the wood. Even to this day it has been a great fascination as to how the Celts were able to forge the steel into the perfect ring size and then place it on the wooden frame and not fall off. Later when we examine the making of their swords will we discover what the trick was to the skill they had when it came to forging metals.

In the national museum of Copenhagen is there one of the best preserved examples of a Celtic wagon. Judging from the beautiful gold art work on it, it was likely used as part of a burial ceremony. When we recall the burial site of Hochorf in Austria, Celts often buried with the deceased many of the artifacts of his life and that often included his chariot or wagon. The wagon was elaborately decorated for the occasion, as the example found in the Copenhagen museum shows.

Again when you simply look at the wagon you get the same sense as before it must have been a very bumpy ride for those riding it. Once again this is not the case. The wagon bed rested on two short extended bars from the two axels. The front bars were hitched to the harness extension so it could move up and down according the ground elevation. Further, the most important feature was the fact the short bars were not rigid and thus again absorbed the shock of the rough terrain. As it turns out the Celts were very much aware that because they did not have roads like the Romans they made their vehicles to anticipate the inconsistent surfaces. Thus now having seen the type of ingenuity of the Celts we can comprehend how it was they could move so swiftly not only their people so incredibly far but also their war wagons.

The Celtic Sword

Probably the greatest example of Celtic metallurgy is their fighting sword. This near four foot long weapon with its signature slightly extended width in the centre and ornamental hand grip was amazement to the people of the time as well as to engineers today. Again, Julius Caesar had his blacksmiths examine the weapon to learn its secrets and it the end they had no success duplicating it. The trick in the making of the weapon was simply the patience of forging, smelting, and re-bending the iron to which it came to be the closest example of steel we understand today. It was a labour of love to make the perfect sword. The Roman sword by comparison was indeed a well crafted iron weapon: sturdy, strong and very heavy. The problem is it was only forged and smelted once in the process. However, by changing their military tactics to make the weapon a swifter tool to maneuver, shortening its length was the key to its success. Yet it did irk them to think the Celtic sword was a better quality device in workmanship then theirs and something they never mastered.

Original Celtic swords can be found in just about every museum across Europe and even museums in North America, like New York and Toronto. Yet Roman swords on the other hand I have yet to see one anywhere. On the internet even you may come across one or two examples of the poor remains of a Roman sword; however, a Celtic sword you will find in the hundreds.

In some cases they look so new it is hardly believable the sword is over 2000 years old. It is a modern day testimonial to the Celtic craftsmanship.

Chapter 4

Druids

"Honour the gods, do no evil, and practice bravery."

Diogenes Laetes, 2nd century

D ruids were the proclaimed sinister people of the Celtic world and the ones often accused of having the crazed mentality of fighting warriors. The stories of this secretive religious cult are in the thousands, especially within the church. Druids were readily recognized as part of the higher political infrastructure of the Celtic society. In Caesar's Gaul campaign he made no mistake in identifying the Druids as the key to the Celtic people. By destroying them he would conquer the Celts both in mind and spirit. It would appear after an exhaustive study on the point it did have merit. Druids were consulted on daily decision making by the kings. As such they did have enormous political power in the tuathe (provinces). In the historical events around Boudicca and

Vercingetorix's rebellions, both consulted with Druids. In legend, King Conchobar McNessa consulted with Cathbad and Queen Medt consulted with her Druid before she attacked Ulster. However, regardless how history has for the most part demonized them, the real truth is they were for the most part a scholarly mix of physicians, historians, lawyers, and bards.

The Druids; where did they come from? Who were they? How was it possible for them to have created such a fascinating mystery around them like the more than famous great Merlyn of King Arthur? And more importantly were they really as powerful as the folklore would have us believe?

Once again, we have to start with actual archaeological evidence to begin the process of understanding this strange sect of the Celts. If we start with numerous Greek historians of the Celts, there are virtually no references to the Druids of the Celts in the Mediterranean world. In fact we find that even in Galatia where Saint Paul has written dozens of letters, again, no mention of the mysterious shamans. In fact when Tacitus traveled across Gaul into Germany he too made no mention of the druids either. Shoning of Alexandria traveled through Iberia and Britain c. 150 BC. He claims there were only Druids found in Briton. Thus in all the known written records of the time, from 500 BC to 75AD, the physical evidence of Druids is sparse. Julius Caesar it turns out is our first big source from which to learn what part of Europe the Druids primary existed in and give us our first big idea where they may have come from. He however, has the Druids restricted to Gaul and Briton and nowhere else.

This point is backed up by T.D. Kendrick in his book *The Druids*.

In other writings like Strabo and Pompenius Mela, there is a confirming reference from Julius Caesar's writing that the druids origin (or main centre) was on an island in Britain. Britainwas by several sources of the time the identifiable place for the Druid order. Tacitus too makes the reference of an island in Britain. Finally when we look at one of the great Celtic legends, the Tan Bo the training of Cuchalain was on the Druid Island east of Ireland. Historians generally feel it was the Island of Man. However, there is very little archaeological evidence to support this. It would seem Anglesey of Wales is the most probable place especially when later archaeology in 1943 does provide the best proof that this is so. The finds have confirmed that Druids go back in this region as far back as 1500 BC.

In archaeology, experts for the most part associate the Druids with the thousand of stone formations across Europe especial the world renowned Stonehenge in England. If that is the case then we know that two things come to light. The first one is that the stone circles of Europe were developments of the Urnfield people and the second is that stone formations exist primarily in Western Europe. Examining the burials of Hochdorf and the Princess of Vix there was found little evidence of Druid rituals at the sites. In Denmark with its famous Gundtsrup Cauldron, we have our first real evidence of Druid existence. Curnonus, the famous Celtic god of forest, is clearly engraved on the cauldron. Thus we know from the physical evidence the Druid influence was from Gaul up to Denmark and accepting the stone circles as another source, then into Britain and Ireland. This is one of those situations where as the Celts migrated across Europe they picked up the customs of the people they settled with. Based on the dates (1500 BC) the Druids as Urnfield cultural source would be very ominous assimilation with the Celts. From what has been learned of them as an adaptable cult, it wouldn't be hard to believe they easily assimilated themselves into the Celtic society quickly.

The makeups of the Druids were not conducive to the Celtic world, especially in the Hallstatt age. The Celts, were a nomadic people. When we study the composition of Druids they could only have existed in a more permanently located society and the Urnfield were definitely that by 500 BC. As much as the Romans tried to dismiss them as simple shamans, it turns out they were anything but. In Caesar's writings as was later confirmed by Tacitus, it took twenty years of study to become a full Druid. What they studied in brief was astrology, history, biology, music, poetry, rhetoric, Brehon law, Ogham, and finally politics. To be able to study in such depth, they needed to be in a settled society as were the Urnfield people. Just one more reason why it wasn't possible the Druids could have originated with the mobile Celts.

Stonehenge

As mentioned the stone circles of Western Europe and the British Islands were all built by the Urnfield people. They are not Celtic in any sense at all. The Druids seems to have had an enormous amount of knowledge on the stones and their use; which only adds yet another piece of evidence to their origins. As much as some sources say the stone circle like Stonehenge were used for rituals or , ceremonial practices, it turns out in the latest studies this is not the case at all. The stone circles in all their different assorted designs were primarily all burial sites. Further in every aspect they followed Urnfield practices and not Celtic. For example in every stone circle was found the remains of a cremated body. Newgrange in Ireland is said to be one of the best examples of this. A dig of Stonehenge in 2005 also confirmed numerous graves of cremated remains. Only in one example was there an actual body found in the far outer ridge circling the stone formation. Druids have been placed at stone circles by various sources like Tacitus and Pomponious Mela, but almost nothing was said of their activity. It seems the

Druids had very little to do with the stone formations; thus the validity of recent evidence to the ritualistic claim is being dismissed.

There's no proof as of yet, but it does seem that when the Celts did assimilate the Druids to their beliefs. The Druids adapted and changed their processes of ritualistic practices especially when it came to burials. The Celts did not cremate their dead but instead buried them. Further the Celts did not bury their dead in huge monoliths stone burials. Celts preferred to bury their own in basically unmarked grounds near a sacred centre like a stream or river. As in the Hotchdorf tomb Celts buried their dead with a large number of artifacts including the deceases horse and in the odd occasion his personal slave.

When you consider the lengthy training it took to become a Druid it is not surprising they should become adaptive to their new masters. In fact they may very well have added a few of their own rituals in the process; Ogham and stone carvings seems the most likely examples. Stones carvings don't appear in the Celtic world until 400 AD. Therefore it's likely that's when the Druids started to make their mark on the Celts. Up until that point bronze was the preferred material of religious or ceremonial art.

Ogham is a notch marking letter system. As mentioned it is seen on the edges of pillar stones. There are four groups of 5 notches. 'Ogham' means 'trees' in Gaelic, so each of the marks represents a tree. Each tree has of course a certain importance, the Oak tree is said to have the highest hour of them all. The shrub trees are said have the least importance and some even considered being bad luck. As such the way the markings are applied it can be interpreted as a simple message like the name of a place or applied as a magical spell. As can be tell each tree mark also stands for a letter this is how words are formed. However, be aware the Druids did not use these words in sentences. A single word was notched out on a side of a stone and that's all there was to it. The importance of Ogham was for the most part ritualistic and it is still regarded in this fashion much today. You can figure out the rituals or divination works by simply understanding the importance of trees are to the Celt.

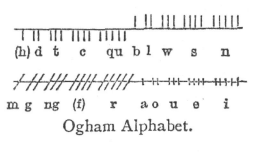

Ogham Alphabet.

Ogham

Closely examining the Druids for what they were you can see the extent of their knowledge and as stated it wasn't possible this knowledge could have come from being a mobile society as the Celts were right up to about 400 BC, and again, once the La Tène period got well underway. The Great Brennus and his sacking of Rome and Dephi is an example how the Celts with far more aggression expand into the east of Europe.

As mentioned to become a Druid it was a twenty year study period. The learning process was from all memory; nothing was written. When you get into some of their medicine, spells, and curses there was good reason for it. Nothing was real unless it followed certain rules. This prevented a commoner from issuing a curse to anyone without authority. In terms of the practice of medicine with herbs it was especially critical that it be done right or else the patient may very well become a victim instead of healing. When we go into the areas of season prediction which was very essential to the farmers it was critical they be accurate. Lastly, according to both historical events and the great legends, giving bad advice to a king could very well cost a Druid his life, and in Gaul and Briton it did. Thus getting the training right took lots of time and it was done in meticulous fashion.

Twenty years of training is a lot time and when there are no books to study from a method of training to retain the information had to have been in place; and rightly so. It turns out the method was through poetry. Everything was done in a poetic verse or as some would call 'bard.' The Irish monks provide us with the best example of how it all worked. The best example of the poetic bard was the great Tan Bo Bard. It was written down for the first time around the 7th century AD. The whole thing is a huge poem. There is almost no general dialogue in the entire story. The great aspect of the poem is that it is likely the story as it was first spoken, and has retained its original form for centuries. Unlike a common story which can be easily embellished as the years go by, in a poem it's much harder to do that, especially if you are not very good with rhyme. When you see some of the legends that have come down through the ages in their format its fascinating to think they are likely in their original state from when they were first spoken. As can be told this is how the druids were able to keep everything they learned in proper order. Further it gives it credibility that the story is true to its origins.

The poetic format was of course expanded to medicine, law, history, and of course bards for plain and simple entertainment. Brian Boru of 9th century Ireland is said to have learned over a hundred bards by the time he was just 11 years old. It gives you an idea just how important the poetic form was to the communication systems of the time. Which brings up the next point of the Druids' order; there were threes levels to their hierarchy system. The first level was Bard, the second level was Brehon, and the third was Fili. When you mastered all three levels you graduated to wearing the white robe as Druid. A Bard was a musical Druid, primarily in the role of entertainment; sometime in Wales this was referred to as a talisman. A Brehon was a circuit lawyer-judge. He provided legal counsel and decision on legal matters. A Fili is a divinations Druid, who specialized in predictions and was very close to becoming a full honoured Druid. It was very important that his observations were accurate.

Now seeing we are at this level of understanding of the Druids, we can we can now explore some of the things modern science has shown of their great magic. In astronomy for example there is not a lot of mystery there. If you sit down for any length of time just watching the stars and the sun you will start to notice patterns. One of the big signatures of the Druids is their exceptional knowledge of the rising sun in the east. The most fascinating example of this is New Grange in Ireland. On an exact day in April, every year, the sun light for fifteen minutes shine through to the centre of the tomb. It's a huge tourist attraction to the country and well worth the money to see. Stonehenge is said to offer a similar example where the two stones on the east side of the circle exactly lined up on that given day that sun light shines perfectly through the centre. Now when you have had twenty years to examine this phenomenon, it comes as no surprise to understand the mechanics of it all. Next, on a more simply note, the Druids knew the moon rises once every month. As such they had the fundamentals of a calendar year. To get a precise reading on a given festival like Beltanee each year they knew certain plant life behaved in a rather accurate manner, like Hawthorn trees. A Hawthorn tree usually blooms on the first of May each year. In Canada it is found to be on May 7th. It is said from the tree if there is any irregularities in the calendar that year, then from the blooming of the tree they make their corrections.

Stonehenge, as has been confirmed numerous times over, was built about 4,000 years ago in south west England. There are two types of stones that make up two circles. The interior large stone are said are blue stones and the shorter ones on the outside are described as white stones. The outer circle was built 200 years after the inner circle was constructed. Both stones have been proven came from the south west part of Wales. What is amazing about this is the consensus is the stones were floated on barges to their present location. How they were erected now was confirmed by a Robert Alkinson (1978) by massive dirt ramps in similar fashions as the Egyptians did in building the pyramids. For the longest time it was believed the Urnfield people built them with wooden scaffolds. In a 2005 archaeological dig it was confirmed that the stone circle was not a ritualistic centre but instead a massive burial ground. All this spring solstice stuff that is presently going around Stonehenge is now proven to be sheer nonsense.

Celtic Religion

From here it would seem that to understand the role of the Druids in the Celtic community you have to have some idea of their religion and beliefs. The Celtic god pantheon is in the hundreds, and trying to sort through them all you will never seem to know what the order is at all. Miranda Green in her study of the Celtic deities seems to come the closest to knowing their origins. From archeological finds in southern France and in Denmark the 7-spoke wheel carvings have at last has revealed that the Celts first worshipped the sun. This can be dated back to the Hallstatt age. From this you can see later how the sun plays a role in their burial ceremonies.

From here it would seem the Celt's gods evolved to animal or natural forms like the boar, the deer, the salmon, the horse, he raven, even trees. Somewhere in the middle period of the La Tène period the gods started to take human forms. Scholars are of the consensus that the Etruscans had the most influence in this change. As it is many of the gods are named to be representative of various animals, like Epona, Goddess of the horse. The horse goddess was to the Celts a very important deity; considering the Horse was a prized animal in their culture.

Eventually the Gods took on human forms and stood for themselves in much the same way as the Roman and Greeks gods did. Again sorting through them all was difficult. Caesar in his writings could only compare them to Roman gods. He was convinced that the god Mercury was the most popular of the all the Celtic gods. Mercury is symbolized with lightning bolts. It turns out after Rome took over Gaul the Celts, when again making their religious icons, used the 7 – poke wheel (symbolizing the sun), now accompanied by lightning bolts. Thus there does seem to be evidence of a genuine comparison. The Celtic god that Caesar was making comparisons to was the (Gaulic Celt) god Artaios. Artaios was similar god to that of brigid the god of the arts and commerce. As can be seen Caesar didn't quite fully understand the Celtic deity system.

As mentioned because there are so many gods in the Celtic pantheon it is felt the same god is called by many different names. An example of this is Brighid (Goddess of fire); in Gaul she is referred to as Brigandua. As to the order of the Gods Dagda (the Good God) appears to be the most prominent. His female counterpart or partner is Dana (the mother Goddess). Her name comes up a lot in Irish and Welsh folklore. Often the people who settled in Ireland circa in 350 BC are referred to as the Tuatha De Dana. Next comes Lugh, he is said to be the most popular of the Celtic diety. It is felt he may have been misinterpreted by Caesar to be a comparison of Mercury. Lugnasad (August 1) is in his Honour. In Northern Irish circles he has a significant role in many of their legends. Next is Manannan Mac Lir (Son of the Sea). His name gets mentioned a lot in Breton, Wale,s and Ireland. From here are two popular deities that makes perfect sense when the

Celts had such a high regard for the wild: Cernonus the horned god of nature and Arduine the hunting goddess. The French Ardennes region is named after her. Here is a summary of the most common Celtic Gods:

- Dagda of the Tuatha de Danaan – Supreme god, represented by all triad forms.
- Lugh – The god of many talents.
- Boinn – The sacred goddess of water, Boyne River named after her.
- Cernonus – Horn God of the wild, protector of all wild life.
- Bellanus – God of cures and figurine offerings.
- Sequana – Gaulic goddess of the sacred waters, Seine river named after her.
- Epona – Goddess of the horse.
- Morrigan – War goddess, represented by the raven.
- Mananan – God of the sea.
- Brigid – Worship at Imbolc, goddess of poem, healing and smithcraft.

Worship practices

Lucan, the poet in the 1st century, makes one of the earliest references to the Celtic practices. As mentioned the Celts did not have a structural centre like a church or altar to practice their beliefs by. Lucan points out the Celts generally gathered in the deep woods near a stream or river. What he describes is a practice that was often a sacrifice of some description, and which often turned gory. The Druid was the centre of the ceremony and it would seem if the sacrifice was human it was something to do with getting a divination for good hunting or a crop.

This has been confirmed from the examinations done of the Man of Lindow Moss in Cheshire and the Tullund man in Denmark up near Arhus. Both bodies were found to have hazelnuts in their stomachs with berries. Both victims had been struck over the head with a blunt object and their necks garroted by rope. Further examination of the bodies uncovered that victims were of persons of high importance, possibly a prince or even a tuathe king.

When it came to animals being sacrificed it was divination of the outcome of an immediate event, say a battle, or it was for an inauguration, perhaps of a king. What was reported out of both Wales and Ireland was when a horse or bull was killed it was a ceremonial for a new ruler. Saint Finian of Ireland described one such ceremony where the new king had drink the blood of a bull so he became one with the animal and thus worthy to rule the province. Again the symbolism of animals in the ceremony was always important.

Like every culture even today there were major festival seasons with the Celts and of course they aligned with deities. Samhaine (November 1) was by far the most important festival of the year it symbolized the end of the summer season and the beginning of winter. It was celebrated primarily of the god Lugh for the festival commemorated a variety of subjects, like harvest and the conclusion of all contracts. However the big one was of course the recognition of the sprits from the other world. Today this date event is now called Halloween.

The second great festival is Imbolc (Feb 1), meaning "around the belly;"; it is in honour of Brigid, who is the goddess of healing, poetry, smithcraft and the sacred flame. A candle is lit to permanently burn to mark the midpoint in the winter season. The ice candle is said to have originated from this festival. In practically the winter stores may have been depleted and possibly disease had broken out from some stores going bad. A sign of hope was now needed and Imbolc was it.

Imbolc, I find, is an interesting time of activities in the crannog. As mentioned it's a time marked on the Celtic calendar when the household took stock of everything. It was hoped there would be a birth either in the animal stock or in the family. If so this was a sign of good luck, not to mention an increase in the family size and natural wealth of the community. When a child was born than he/she is circled around the fire three times; known as the baptism of fire. This was later replaced with the Christian tradition of water baptism. For the little community a similar general ritual was carried out where a Brigid effigy was made and everyone together circled the crannog three times as a blessing to it as well.

The third big festival is Beltane (May 1st), which means "bell fire," symbolizing new beginnings and fertilization, and it really was a special occasion for this is when the farmers let out their livestock to at last graze in the open fields. Prior to doing this the livestock needed to be blessed. The Celts made two long lines of fire and the farm animals would parade between them. Beltanes was named in honour of the god Beltanus. Druids had to be very careful to get this date right for the rest of the calendar year was marked by it. As mentioned earlier the Druids wait for the budding of the hawthorn to mark the actual day. Apparently a Saxon tradition has evolved from this day as well and that is the Maypole tradition.

As many will know Beltane is seen as a time of what appears to be as a wild orgy. By our standards today that is quite surprising, but it has to be understood these are a different people and a different time. They were not a society inhibited by what has become recognized as Victorian modesty.

As such here is how a typical Beltane Celtic festival was carried out. As mentioned the Druids would not be watching the moon for the changing of the season, but would be watching when the hawthorn first bloomed into flower. This was the signal for everyone to put out their regular community fires and wait for the Ard-Ri at the nation's capital like Tara in Ireland to light the first Beltane fire. Once lit, fires were seen being lit across the land. It really would have been seen as quite an impressive sight. From here young naked men and women would jump over the fire in celebration. They would than roll in the grass dew and dunk their heads in spring water as sign of purification. After they would pick flowers and make head garlands for the females, and then run off into the bushes and consummate their new love. Unlike the Romans who actually did engage in public orgies, especially during Caligula's time, for the Celts other than dancing nude in public the actual act of sex was a very private event between lovers.

Finally the last big religious festival is Lugnasad (August 1st). To the Celts Autumn started in August and it was called "Lommas" which means "first loaf." This is a celebration most experts strongly feel had its origins with the Urnfield culture and was simply added into the Celtic practices. Of course the festival was in honour of Lugh. It was celebrated with sport, weddings and the commitment to any contracts that were promised. A contract was ratified when a brooch was given to the lender. Further if there were any warriors on campaigns, this is the time they would return home to start work on the harvest. This celebration, unlike the others, went on for a fortnight of primarily eating and drinking. The impression I get from this is all the previously stored food was consumed to make way for the new; for the actual harvesting did not occur until after the celebration was conducted.

Lugh full name is "Lugh Lamfada," meaning "light of the long arm." His nickname was commonly known as "Lewy the long arm." His legendary story says that when he tried to gain entrance to King Nuada's court at Tara, admission was granted when it was proven he was the god that had mastered the talents of all men.

When the festival at last came to its end everyone would go out to harvest. The first cut was given to the gods as one last piece of celebration before the hard work began. Here a huge circular dance was performed and in this case it was in honour of Cernonus the god of the wild. Yes, there was also the last hunt of the season to be conducted as well, along with the harvest.

Summary of the seasons and measuring time

In terms of the festivals there was real sense of order in the Celtic community. First they had a sense of time and from it they clearly knew the seasons; they were quite capable of preparing for them especially winter. They knew they had to start seriously working on the feed for their livestock and family come August and hopefully everything was done by November 1st. All the indications seem to point that if they did not properly prepare for the winter by February it would show, and they would hope that Brigid could help them out. Finally with Lughnasad we get the impression that the Celts did have a sense of business. The same line of thinking we have today for loans had did too; however, their business dealings only lasted for a few months when the loan had to be fully paid back. The Druids realized from simply keeping track of the moon activities that it appeared twelve times. From there it was simple case of watching nature at the

certain counts of the moon when each season started. Beltane was said to be the most important for it was more or less the gauging point for the rest of the year. Druids could figure out how much they were on or off by when the hawthorn bloomed.

The Celtic Legal System and Druids

Who had the real authority over the people was a subject that Julius Caesar had a great deal of interest in. He needed to know who was calling the shots. As it was he in his so-called careful examination missed out on how it all really worked. Yes, the head Druid no doubt played a big role in the legal system of the Celts and was seen to have the ultimatedecision-making power. The truth is that discipline was for the most part conducted at the local level and thus the allegiance was sworn to the tuathe monarch rather than at the national stage.

As mentioned, the Brehons where a kind of mobile lawyer/judge so to speak. In practice they really didn't make decisions on disputes but merely quoted the laws.

From the situation it was easy to tell who was at fault and if both parties were going to fallow the law then they knew how it was to be resolved. The person at fault was encouraged to do what was right by the Brehon rather being ordered like a judge would do in a modern day court. Where a matter required a jury so to speak, an assembly of "freemen" was called upon. Freemen were a class down from warriors, the group usually made up of farmers, blacksmith, craftsmen, and bards. Here though when a decision was made it was binding. If the guilty party refused to respect the decision than the plaintiff had the right to seek compensation on his own. There was no appeal in any decisions made.

What Caesar saw in terms of the judiciary system was the high Druids' part in the final decision. If a matter was considered a serious case such as murder, the penalty was left to the Druid to decide upon. The Druid played no role in determining the guilty party but did decide the fate of the accused. From this Caesar concluded the Druids were the main party in all legal situations.

Brehon law was broken down into two groups: Senchós Mor (civil law) and Acail (criminal law). The laws did not come from legislation but from a consensus of Druids and Brehons at a gathering normally on Samhain. Brehons were paid was usually 1/12th the value of the disputed property's worth.

The last piece of legal process in the Celtic society was how their monarchs came to power. Again, the Celts did not have a central order as was recognized in the Roman world. Their society evolved from the tuathe level. Tuathe Kings could inherit their throne, hence the clan system that still exists in both Scotland and Ireland. However, at the provincial and national level the Kings were elected. Vortigern and Vercingetorix are two such examples of leaders being elected. Also, unlike the Norman system the tuathe kings were not necessarily bound to the call of their provincial ruler. If a local tuathe monarch did not want to participate in an armed conflict he was free to opt out. Mind you that often meant retaliation later for disloyalty, but it was not illegal.

CHAPTER 5

The Celtic Empire

"Brennus and his army were now faced by the
Greeks who had mustered at Delphi....
No good were sent by the God....
For the ground occupied by
the Gaulic army was shaken violently.."

PAUSANIS

At the peak of the Celtic expansion in 250 BC virtually the whole of Europe was occupied by this single culture. As such many claim that the Celts actually achieved empire status. Here we are going to take a look at how they did it and the principle aspects that allows them to be recognized as an empire.

We have become accustomed to thinking that empires are those that are only possible when under a single ruler such like Alexander the Great of the Macedonian Empire, Julius Caesar of the Roman Empire, and

Napoleon Bonaparte of the French Empire. The idea an empire existing in an associate conglomerate of states does not readily enter our modern imagination, like the Austrian-Hungarian Empire of 1912. Yet as with this one example empires can exist in a group like confederacy. The Iroquois were declared an empire in the 16th century because of the land area they controlled after defeating the Huron. The Iroquois nation stretched from the New York state through much of Quebec and southern Ontario. Yet the Iroquois were made of 5 major tribes like the Mohawks and the Senecas. Therefore, it is in the academic line of thinking that based on an *aggressive line of expansion* by a single group of people, being declared an empire is a plausible.

Therefore, the Celts in the La Tène period were definitely of an age of *aggressive expansionism*. As was mentioned earlier, the Celts had a great cultural revolution circa 350 BC. They went from a standard kingdom to a warrior based community. If they were an aggressive people in the Hallstatt age, they were even more so now. The Celtic nation stretched basically through the whole of Western Europe and was bordered by the Rhine and the Italian Alps in the east. Archaeological evidence has shown the Celts were a prosperous people and growing in physical size. As such another massive expansion took place, this time now into regions of Europe that was settled by cultures that were supposedly at a superior, more advanced level of development.

Many authors who discuss this time period don't really give you any sense of this unique period only that for the next hundred or so years it went on and that it was basically a simple continuation of the Hallstatt period, which is not true at all. The expansion age of the Hallstatt period started around 500 BC and slowly migrated west to around 400 BC. There are no stories either in the Celtic legends or officially written by people like Aristotle or Plato of an empire like behaviour of Celtic expansion. Nor is there any evidence in archaeology either. In the first period of the Celts' existence they simply migrated and absorbed the people they took over; in this case it was the Urnfield people.

However, starting in 400 BC it was quite a different story. Going into nations like Greece and Etruria there was plenty of people about to record their exploits. It turns out the migration was clearly a lot more violent, and historians like Livy have recorded many of the battles that took place in this massive expansionism. If we start with the occupation of the Po valley as the beginning and moving to being employed by the Egyptians (c. 200 BC) as mercenaries marking the end of the Celtic Empire, than it's fair to say the empire's age was about 200 years. All the evidence seems to suggest that they peaked at about 220 BC with the Carthage Empire now beginning to taking land away from them in southern Spain (Iberia).

Suddenly the Celts take on a much more prominent role in world history when very few empires have lasted this long. You have to remember the Celtic empire period began after Western Europe was already taken. If we are to include the Hallstatt age as well then the Celts then they are equal with the Romans. The Roman Empire was not declared until after Julius Caesar's time and if 400 AD marked the end of the empire than both the Celts and the Romans has about the same time period of 400 years.

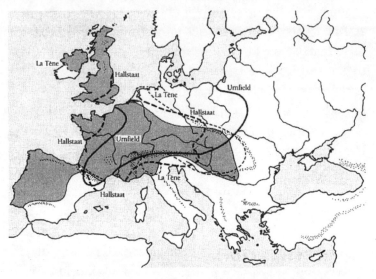

The extent of the Celtic Empire illustration

The Celtic Warrior

The La Tène age was the defining point to the Celts' new mentality as a people. Their becoming a warrior based society was reported by such people like Livy, Tacitus, Aristotle and even Plato. Their frame of mind was even more aggressive than ever. You might say they were a society that could very well be paralleled to the Spartans. Physical fitness was compulsory for everyone and from the legends in Ireland reported by the monks in the 7th century, the youth both male and female started training early in life. Allowing yourself to become overweight was a punishable offence. Next came the subject of simple bravery. Their religion had evolved to the point where they did not believe they could die, not completely. Apparently they believed that their soul would simply go into another body when killed on the battlefield or if taken to Tir Nanog (their heaven) you could ask Lugh to return to earth. The story of Ossin (Finn McCool's son) is an example of this belief.

Next we come to the weapons of the Celts. The basic military weaponry was a long slashing sword and large oval wooden shield. The sword, as previously mentioned, was actually a very well made iron-steel weapon. Even to this day it is said to have been a superior to anything made in the Mediterranean states including Rome. The wooden shield though proved to be their down fall especially against the Romans. From here if the warrior could afford it he would have a conical shape helmet and if a captain of sort would be distinguished with an animal like figure on top of it. Archaeologists have found helmets with boars, ravens, and bulls in them as a few examples of the Celtic head wear.

As for clothing, this has been a considerable topic of discussion. It would seem in many examples the Celts did not wear anything when they went into battle. Cicero was the first to mention this in his first encounters with the Celts in battle. Again we hear more of it with Julius Caesar in Gaul and Tacitus in Britain. This was accompanied by the fact the Celts would do up their hair in long spikes using lime and their bodies sometime covered in blue tattoos. With you add in their terrifying screams as they ran across the field it was in many a situation unnerving to the enemy.

The Celtic battle format apparently was quite simple and through the ages never changes much. It was to be their undoing once they started going up the discipline formations of the Romans. The army would form up with the Chariots up front in a long line. Behind them were the huge masses of infantry. On either flank were their cavalry units. The strategy of going into battle was started with the chariots charging head long into the enemy front ranks. To the enemy it appeared they wear going to rip through their line and as such would be unnerved and break rank to avoid being hit. If they did the chariots would keep on going. If they held as was often the case with the Romans, just at the last moment they would swerve off and the charioteer would throw a spear into the enemy ranks. Hopefully the fear was enough to cause some confusion and thus the charging infantry right behind the charioteer would take advantage of and in massive weight smash head on into the ranks of the enemy. In the early years of fighting the Romans this technique actually did work, because at the time the Romans had only two files from which to hold off the Celtic onslaught. From here the flanking cavalry would charge and try to circle in behind the enemy. This part of the battle was for the most part the most successful and found to be an effective part of the Celtic strategy for well over a hundred years. Countries that did employ

Celtic mercenaries like the Greeks did, the cavalry attacks was proven the best aspect to their fighting ability.

The Celts on the March

The name Brennus seems to always pop up as the starting point of the great Celtic invasions of the Mediterranean nations. It would seem a number of historians didn't take the time to realize that there were two of them in the great empire age and got confused when trying to describe the man in two major events of the Celtic wars. The first Brennus is legendary for having attacked Rome circa 390 BC. This Brennus was the most amazing for he showed the full extent of the Celtic manpower to steam roll over the Romans. Evidence showed he clearly had a mass army of over 250,000 warriors. The sheer size of the force was an easy matter to sacking the city. The second Brennus occurred in 281 BC when he attacked Delphi, the religious capital of the Greeks. Brennus (II) only had an army of some 40,000. The force was not large enough that the Greeks couldn't eventually repel it, which they did, and Brennus (II) ended up committing suicide as a result of the disgraceful conduct.

Scene of Celts in combat illustration

What both men represented was the new age of Celts who were on the march and what we are about to see is the extent to which they were.

The occupation of the Po Valley in 400 BC was the first big push. The Celts that made this big move were the Arveni, Senones, Aedui, Boi, and the Carnutes. Coming over the alpines in one massive surge they crashed into their longtime trading partners, the Etruscans. The Etruscans proved to be no match and in a diagonal line the Celts occupied an enormous strip of land from Italy that almost reached Rome itself. For nearly a hundred years the Celts went on raids into the south sacking both Etruscan and Roman settlements with almost no opposition. The devastation was such that historians today declared that with the Romans now expanding north themselves, Etruria ceased to exist by the year 300 BC. The Italian boot was basically now cut in half, with the

Celts in the north and the Romans in the south. It was not until 225 BC that the Romans were able to finally check the Celtic influence in the region in the Battle of Telemon. For the first time do we see Roman military organization start to take true form. However, be aware that northern Italy had been occupied by the La Tène Celts for the previous 150 years. This is not a short period of time to be easily dismissed as some writers try to do.

According to the writings of Pompius Trogus, the next big Celtic move happened in 360-355 BC when an aggressive migration pushed south east into what are now Hungary, Bulgaria, and Romania. In fact it was claimed by Russian historians this migration went as far as the Crimea, so it was a massive push that involved hundreds of thousands of Celts. And staying with the region we will leap just a little further into the future and note that in 200 BC on, another push went in the Carpathian Basin of Russia. So when we now look at the Celtic map, overlapping both the Hallstatt and the La Tène Celts, the Celtic empire now stretched from the beaches of Portugal all the way to the shores of the Crimea and from northern Scotland all the way down to the Po Valley of Italy.

And of course it still does not end here. In 278 BC two major Celtics tribes, the Tectosages and the Tricomi, marched into the area now known as Turkey. There is however some debate on this for many feel the Celts were invited in much the same way as the Saxons were invited into Briton by Vortigern, circa 420 AD. What has now become well known today as Galacia in the northern half of Turkey is where the Celts settled. From here they accepted employment as mercenaries by Nicodemus, King of the Pergarnums.

The La Tène culture that pushed west, being of a different mentality, came into confrontation with Halstatt Celts. There is not much written on this but Caesar seems in his writing to give us the best evidence when it came to the tribes respecting one another. Only when it is in their best interest would Celts get along with one another. An example is when the five major tribes migrated into the Po Valley (290 BC). It was in their best interest to cooperate fighting the Etruscans, and so they did. However, later we find the Boi tribe did not get along with the other four and feuding began; using this as a reference explains how the Gauls did not completely align against Caesar and proved they were not a consistent people. Thus when we see that the La Tène spread into Western Europe it is understood it was not accomplished without a fight.

The La Tène culture spread into Gaul and Briton, but not into Iberia (Spain). Evidence of the La Tène culture was found recently in the north east of Spain but it was learned that this happened as result of the Romans push in Gaul. The Aquitonis were found to have migrated into Iberia and settled just inside the Pyrenees mountain range. This is as far as the La Tène culture makes it into Iberia.

The Start of the Decline

Between 283 and 265 BC, feuds between singular tribes caused migration, along with mercenary expeditions to spread their influence around the Mediterranean. The Celtic unity was clearly breaking down at this point in time. For example, in the Po Valley the Boi tribe got themselves into ten serious conflicts with the surrounding

Cisalpine Celts. The conflicts drained a lot of manpower, and when the Romans started appearing there was not the unity that once existed under Brennus (I). In terms of mercenaries, the Celts in the thousands hired themselves out to the Spartans, Pergarnums, Macedonians, and Egyptians. These four nations (so to speak) were at constant war with their neighbors and in the process the Celts were decimated. This is the turning point in the Celtic Empire, for after this everything starts to decline.

The point from which the decline starts is at the Battle of Telamon just 9 miles north of the city of Rome in 225 BC. Here in a pincer move the Romans have their first big military battle against a Celtic Army of 70,000. The Celts should have won the battle by their sheer size but fighting naked against an army Romans in armour they were easily slaughtered.

The victory gave the Romans the confidence where they started their own invasion of the Po Valley. In a series of attacks the Romans completely occupy the valley by the end of 220 BC and in doing so now have control of all the boot of Italy.

Also, in North Africa another empire is rising and it is the empire of Carthage. While the Romans were attacking the Celts in Northern Italy the Carthaginians were attacking the Celts in southern Iberia. By 220 BC the entire strip of shore line of the Iberian Peninsula was under Carthage's control.

It was in this time frame (230 BC) the first Punic War broke out between Rome and Carthage. The fighting was centered on Sicily and the Mediterranean. Carthage was winning the conflict until it lost a major sea battle of the Aegate Islands. The Romans may have been exhausted from the war or were looking to deal with the Celts to their north (the politics in Rome at this time was unpredictable) decided to end the conflict with a treaty, and Carthage was spared from being destroyed.

As it was over the next few years it was an uneasy peace for the Romans started interfering in the Carthage territory of Iberia. There were a number of small cities that were dominated by a Greek population and the Romans were encouraging the locals to separate. Of course Carthage had to come down on this and thus took military action to suppress the potential uprising. The Greeks in turned looked to Rome for support and thus the second Punic War broke out in 220 BC.

In this conflict the Hannibal of Carthage was the brilliant general the Romans came unbelievably close to losing to. Hannibal raised actually a small army in southern Iberia. It barely accounted for some 20,000 men. They were a mix of Libyans, Carthaginians, and the southern half of Iberian Celts. This was hardly a force against his Roman rival Publius Scipio, who amassed an army of over 85,000. The odds in the beginning looked grievously bad for Carthage. However, brilliant leadership and an unplanned alliance with more Celts soon turned the tables.

When Hannibal set out on his march across southern Gaul in 219 BC with his famed 15 elephant army, he came across with Arverni Celts. When the Arvernis learned he was in pursuit of attacking the Romans they joined his ranks and helped him get over the Alps. It is said Hannibal's ranks swelled to over 45,000. Getting over the Alps in 218 BC he ran into Scipio's army of over 70,000 strong at the Trebia River.

Scipio clearly had the advantage in the initial encounter with Hannibal; however, he had a general who wanted to steal the glory all for himself. The Roman general's name was Sembronius and without orders crossed the river with his own forces. Hannibal was waiting for him. The Roman legions had never seen elephants before used as military weapons and to have 15 of them go charging into their lines they panicked and quickly broke rank. In minutes the battle turned into a route and Scipio had to withdraw from the field.

The Cisalpine Celts were suitably impressed with what they witnessed and Hannibal's army now swelled to over 57,000 strong. With every passing victory Hannibal's army continued to grow.

Hannibal marched his army which was 70% Celtic passed by the city of Rome to a place famously known as Cannae. Here he carefully picked his ground and laid out one of the greatest strategies of any campaign in history. The Romans reorganized and now in greater numbers of 86,000 men, marched confidently straight for Hannibal's camp.

When the Romans arrived they took up their familiar massive three rank style formation. Hannibal had his forces lined up thinly in two ranks but stretched way past the flanks of the Romans. On either side was his cavalry, plus two battalions of infantry hidden from view. The Roman juggernaut marched straight forward what appeared to them was going to be an easy victory. Hannibal is said was standing right in the centre front ranks to greet the onslaught and very slowly moved the centre back as the Roman's advanced. As they did they were not aware the Carthaginian forces were engulfing them. Then to the Roman surprise out of hiding came the enemy's cavalry and flanking infantry. The Romans soon found themselves completely packed into a circle and were now being butchered. It is said Hannibal slaughtered over 47,000 Romans before the day was done. Somehow only 15,000 Romans manage to flee the field. To date historians are all generally agreed this was probably the most impressive battle ever fought in ancient history. To the Celts it was a sweet revenge for the battle of Telamon.

From here complete confusion overtook everyone, for Hannibal decided after this crushing victory not to lay siege to the city of Rome. Hannibal, it is said, offered the city an opportunity to surrender, but the offered was rejected. Maybe the Romans knew Hannibal had not the military engineering skills to take the city, so they decided to risk it, knowing full well their army was all but gone.

From this point on Hannibal's activities become an even greater mystery for he seemed to be marching around aimless around southern Italy with no clear objective. He at last in 216 BC laid siege to two less importance Roman cities for over three years, and wasted away precious man power. After about 8 years of what appeared indecisive leadership the Celts had enough and thus abandoned him. In 203 BC the Romans have finally reorganized and were now threatening Carthage itself. Hannibal with not more than 1800 men left of his once great army was forced to return to Carthage. The following year Carthage capitulated to Rome for a second time.

For the Cisalpine Celts in 202 BC the Romans get their revenge on them as well.

Iberian Campaign

With the fall of the Carthage Empire much of the land in southern Iberian is now taken over by the Romans. For the next hundred or so years; the Romans launched a series of attacks on Iberia which, agonizingly slowly, finally took all of it. The Iberian campaign did not get a lot of historical recording and as such there is this general impression the country fell rather quickly, which was far froma the truth.

> *"Not many of the Cantabri were taken prisoner, for when they saw they lost all hope of freedom, they also lost their desire to preserve their lives, some set fire to their forts and cut their own throats, others willingly died in the flames or took poison..." CASSIO DIO*

Definitely the Iberian campaign was a long, brutal, and sad tragedy; yet it spoke volumes of the Celts and their bravery. In a way it is amazing the Romans were able to endure themselves after coming out of two Punic wars with Carthage.

By 197 BC Rome took full control of southern Iberia. No sooner did they take control when fighting erupted as a result of increased taxes. Typical of the start of the every campaign Roman forces were slaughtered at the Battle of Turda (near what is now Barcelona). A 12,000 man army was defeated to the Turdinian Celts. However, it was a short lived victory. That same year Marcus Helvius slaughtered the Turdinians at Itugi (near the Portugal border). For the near 25 years it was basically a see-saw war with the southern Iberians. Yet, as always, the Romans slowly made their way up to the centre of the country. Fighting was ruthless and the amount of dead on both sides was in the tens of thousands. By 153 BC, despite their impressive forces, the Romans had only managed to take 40% of the interior. The west coast was still in Celtic hands as was the north.

From what is known of the relentless campaign, the year 154 BC must have been Rome's worst nightmare for at now the Lusitanian Celts of the west coast broke out in rebellion. The Lusitanian tribe stretched for much of what we now know as Portugal. The new fighting went on for a solid 5 years. Here it is said the carnage was even worse. The Romans started slaughtering whole communities and forts of all their inhabitants. No one was spared. Needless the say the Celts returned the favour in kind. In the few victories they enjoyed the Romans were mercilessly wiped out. Like Scipio with Hannibal the Romans at last came up with a capable general and his name was Claudius Marcellus. He was able to put an end to the fighting in 150 BC and with that Rome had at last 70% of the country.

Once again, Rome measured out some ruthless taxes to regain their losses from the years of fighting. It did not occur to them that this was what started all the fighting in the first place. As it was another rebellion broke out with the interior Celts in 141 BC.

This rebellion quickly became an embarrassing conflict for the Iberians who were now under a brilliant commander named Viriathus. Viriathus was said to be an even more capable commander then both Brennus of Rome and Vercingetorex of Gaul. He was winning more battles then the Romans were and for once the Romans were on the defensive. In desperation the Romans plotted an assassination to finally get rid of Viriathus and it was successful. No longer with a brilliant leader, the Central Iberians quickly fell apart. The rebellion came to an end circa 130 BC.

All that was left of Iberia is a small section of the North west where there are two major tribes known as the Gallarci and the Austeres. Circa 60 BC the Romans made a final push to take this land from the Celts as well. To their surprise it wasn't all that easy. The Gallarci and Austeres are a vicious and determine people. The fighting goes on in the most savage of manners for over 40 years. Again the Romans find themselves in a very embarrassing situation. How is it possible for such a small piece of territory taking so much of an effort to conquer? Finally, circa 18 BC all of Iberia falls to Rome.

Though there is no mention of it, it does seem very probable that maybe the reason it took the Romans such a long time to win the last remaining piece of Iberia was that starting in 55 BC Rome was also engaged in Gaul with Julius Caesar. When you consider that Caesar; at any given time, had an army of over 50,000 men, that's a lot of resources being used to supply them. It seems especially from the Punic wars the Romans could only support an army of around 60,000 at any given time; thus it's believable the resources for Iberian campaign were likely stripped to the minimum.

The Teutonic Invasion

The Romans at this point in time were not the Celts' only headache. They had problems elsewhere in what was left of their empire. Circa 110 BC out of northern Germany near the Rhine two major tribes the Cimbri and the Teutones started to migrate down into the Cisalpine Celt region which is just north of the Italian Alps. Had they just come and slaughtered off the Celts and went home the Romans would not have paid them any notice. However, this was not the case once they destroyed the Celts in the area they set up their own nation and now became a new menace to the Romans.

In the initial start Rome made a halfhearted attempt to evict the Germans but blundered into a military disaster. Over the next 4 years Roman attempts to remove the invaders all failed miserably. The Teutones and Cimbri after a while became confident in themselves for defeating the Romans became only too easy. They expanded their territory now into the Arverni Tribe region of southern Gaul. As it is the Germans were growing into a mini-empire as more of their countrymen were moving down to join them.

Finally the Romans come up with a competent general named Gaius Marius from Africa. Gaius was a long time seasoned field commander whose trademark was hiring the local inhabitants to fill his ranks. It was a trend that Romans seriously picked up on the declining years of their empire. Gaius was very much aware that the success of the Roman Legions against the northern barbarians was to be as light on the ground as they were. The long slow cumbersome supply wagons that often accompanied the Roman legions he did away with them all. As it was the Romans could move as swiftly to a battle as did the Teutons and the Cimbri.

The new style of tactics took the Germans by surprise. Gaius resorted to a series of fast strikes and ambush technique which were up this point a typical barbarian style of fighting. In about 3 years of fighting Gaius Marius routed the Cimbri and the Teutones from the entire cisalpine region. The door was now open to the one of the most famous Roman campaigns against the Celts in history.

The War in Gaul

By 100-55 BC, the once massive Celtic empire had seriously dwindled. All that was left was central Gaul, Briton, and Hibernia (Ireland). Rome having recently defeating the Greeks took over Asia Minor and of course Galacia went with it. Thus the Celtic influence here that had lasted from 270 BC to roughly 57 BC was over. Surely the Celts would have clued in that they were no longer the once-massive body of people that dominated the whole of Europe and maybe now it's time to unify something like they had under Brennus of Rome. However, following the Iberian campaign we see that the Celts continued their tribal ways of thinking throughout the whole time. The Lusitanias stayed out of the fighting with the Romans until it was too late. This pattern of thinking was to again to repeat itself as the Rome swept across both Gaul and Briton.

At last we have made it to Julius Caesar. So much has been spoken of him previously since of all the Romans military leaders, he wrotethe most. It is from his writings that we learned so much about the behaviour of the Celts, their civilization, and their techniques in battle. Mind you as many historians have pointed out there is an enormous amount of bias and simple miscalculation in his writing, and so you cannot read too much into it.

Unlike Iberia, Gaul collapsed relatively quickly. In fact it did not take Caesar more than 8 years to conquer the whole nation. Unlike the Celts the Romans were continuously improving their methods of fighting. The oval shield for example that Romans used at Cannae were replaced by huge rectangular ones that almost completely covered the soldiers' body. Thus it was not much harder to get access to his body. The simple spear was reshaped into a kind of dishing harpoon. Only part of it was wood and the rest was a long narrow bar with a small hook like head. The object was not to kill anyone with it but to get stuck in the enemy's shield. The weight of the spear would force the enemy to discard it and fight only with a sword. Thus was much easier for the Romans to dispose of him. Lastly the Roman swords were considerably smaller than the long, slashing swords of the Celts. Its design was more of a fast, brief stabbing instrument than anything else.

When you combine the new weapons together in the new Box shape formations the legions took when fighting a foe it all worked very effectively. Celts as a rule, after the chariots flew out of the way, advanced their infantry as a mob. That would cram into the Roman formations and almost no one had room to swing their swords. The Romans on the other hand didn't need the room to jab their small swords through the cracks of their body length shields. It was easy to quickly slice into the body of the Celt squeezed up against his shield. Needless to say the Romans could make fast work of the Celts who in many situations outnumbered the Romans 5 to 1.

Understanding how the military technology seriously shifted in favour of the highly discipline Romans, it's no wonder Caesar was able to make short work of the Gauls.

The campaign against Gaul, it would appear, started all by chance. Everything began when Julius Caesar was Governor of the Roman Territory Cisalpine. As mentioned before after Hannibal the Romans moved into the Alps and completely subdued the Celts once and for all. Circa 61 BC the massive nation of the Helvetii that were living in the now Hungarian region of Europe decided they were going to migrate into Transalpine Gaul via Cisalpine. They were an incredible force of over 350,000. With a force of 60,000 Caesar went out to meet them. It turned into a bloodbath. Within only a few hours (if that) there were only 70,000 of the Celts left. As such the Helvetii returned to where they came from.

As mentioned the Celts were not the most loyal people amongst themselves. They often quarreled with each other and as was fully recorded in the tales of the Tan Bo often stole from one another. This it turned out was of a great conveyance for Julius Caesar, for it was said at the time in his career he had massed a considerable amount of debt and needed a way to get out of it. It turned out the Celts in Gaul would give the relief he needed.

Up near the Belgium border another dispute amongst the Celtic nations erupted. A tribal nation known as the Ebornes was causing the Belgae nation problems. The Belgae asked for assistance from the Romans. In 57 BC Caesar went up with an army of 50,000 Romans to lend the Belgae a hand. Again they made short work of the Ebornes.

From this point on the pattern continued across Gaul. One Celtic nation would attack another and the victim tribe would quickly ask for Roman assistance. In the process Caesar saw his moment to both clear up his debts as well as an opportunity to make a little glory for his political career.

It would appear the Nervii tribe, near the English Channel, was the first to recognize the Roman threat of take over thus started an all-out open rebellion. Unfortunately, none of the neighboring tribes joined them in the revolt and yet another Celting nation came close to extinction as the Romans slaughtered them in the tens of thousands.

However, having said that, the Venittii up in the north-west corner of the now France, too late, broke out in rebellion as well. They unlike the other Celtic nations had a navy with which to fight the Romans with but it was not very large. It is said over a hundred enormous Roman galleons arrived on the scene and made short work of the Venittii as well.

By this point the Romans in 55 BC were now behaving as occupiers. One of the things they were doing as an occupation force was taking grain from the local inhabitants to feed their large army. And seldom if ever did the Romans pay for the grain as well. To say this brought about more angry Gauls is an understatement. What was left of the Nervii nation went to the Germans for help against the Romans. The Germans oblige them and together cross the Rhine in force. Once more the Nervii disregarded the local Celtic nation of the Trevernii in southern Belgium and found them in a local dispute long before they ever met the Romans. The fighting got messy as the Ebornes joined the Trevernii against the Nervii and Germans.

Following this conflict you get a true sense of just how confusing it was to understanding Celtic loyalties. When Caesar at last arrived on the scene the Ebornes changed sides again and were now with the Nervii. They without any support attacked the Romans which was stupid thing to do for again in less than an hour of fighting the Romans slaughter them. Then Caesar drove out the Germans and the Nervii back across the Rhine.

Roman slaughtering of the Celts at long last started to reach its alarming point and so they the Gauls realized if they were going to deal with the Romans it would have to be on an even more massive scale than ever before. And for the first time on a united front the Celts would have to it as well. In 53 BC a major rebellion broke out in central Gaul under the leadership of Vercingeterix of the Arvernii nation. He brought with him the Aulerci, the Senones, the Canutes, the Biturgies, and the Sequauni. Caesar, to fight this massive rebellion, had still only a 50,000 man army.

For the first time he was in well over his head. Yet he was confident that the Gauls were still too fragmented to fight as a single force. Caesar in this line of thinking almost undid him at Gergovia. He thought he had the Gauls all penned in inside a walled fortress only to find it was trap. Behind him was their main army and in minutes he was the one being penned in. Just barely Caesar escaped with his life and what left of his legions raced back to Cisalpine. Vercingeterix was on his heels all the way but called off the pursuit once the Romans were back in their own territory. It was a fatal tactical mistake.

The following year (53 BC) Caesar was back with yet another army and was now the one in hot pursuit of Vercingetorix. The Celts over confident they had driven the Romans off all returned to their respected countries and so were unprepared for the return of the Romans. Vercingeterix was pursued to an infamous fortress Alesia in northwest central Gaul (France). The Celts it turned out took way too long in putting a new force together and as such Caesar was able to build a double wooden ring defence system around the Alesia. Only when it was finished did at last the Celtic horde of over 300,000 shows up to relieve Vercinterix. It was never stated but it is likely the Roman defences were comprised of about 60,000 men, for that seemed the standard size of a roman Army at the time.

The Celts launched their attack at the southwest side of the Defences. Because of their sheer numbers they were making gains into the Roman lines. Yet the Romans stayed to their box formation style of fighting and the Gauls were taking horrible casualties Vercingeterix attacked from the inside and had they persevered it is likely they would have linked up with their counterparts. However, the Roman slaughter machine was taking its toll and the outside attackers broke it off. They swung their attack to the northwest wall near a river and here they met the same kind of Roman butchery as before. Disheartened by the lack of progress and the unbelievable casualties, they broke off the attack. Vercingetrix had no choice to do the same. The next day he surrendered to Caesar and a year later was strangled to death.

Despite the enormous punishment all of Gaul had suffered at the hands of the Romans in 51 BC the Aquitani in southwest Gaul rebelled themselves against the Romans. Needless to say in just a matter of months the Romans crushed the rebellion and thus completely conquered Gaul.

The Final Nail in the Coffin

Britain, unlike Gaul, did not fall readily to the Romans in fact technically it could be argued it was never conquered at all: only subjugated. The reason for this is when the Romans left in 410 AD miraculously the country almost overnight returned to its original state, Celt! So what happened that Britain had quite a different set of circumstances compared to all the other lands they took over and completely Romanized? Well perhaps as some scholars argue it was because of the Iceni rebellion in 61 AD by the famous Boudicca. The rebellion caught the Romans off guard and the consequences destroyed an enormous amount of trade goods and 80,000 lives the Romans could ill afford to lose. The Romans may have found that Britain was just not worth it.

The one thing about Romans has to be remembered is their conquest was all about profits and financial gain. The Carthage wars and the gold that was taken out of Gaul certainly proved that point enough. Britain was a different set of circumstances. They did have gold in this country but nowhere near as much as Gaul; it was primarily an agricultural and tin-based economy. As such the Romans found they have to keep their military expenses to a minimum if they were going to make this occupation work. As such, "client states" were at their highest level here than anywhere else. Being a client state meant you could keep your kingdom and just pay the annual taxes to the Romans. It is from this arrangement the Britons enjoyed a lot more autonomy compared to their counterparts on the continent. The Romans did build in Britain as they did throughout the entire empire, but it was clear from the very beginning there were two major cultures sharing the land.

The start of Roman interest in Britain began in 55 BC when Caesar made his first attempt to invade the island. He was met with disaster and thus he had to abandon the project. The following year he tried again with a bigger force, but apparently the weather played a part with his ships so again he had to prematurely leave.

It's interesting that historians are from this point on very vague as to how the Romans returned to Britain. We suddenly find in 43 D Londinium (London) and Camulodinium (Colchester) are two huge Roman centers with an overall population of 100,000 people. The man who is credited with conquering relatively quickly the southern part of Briton is Aulus Paulinus. He however got bogged down fighting a series of guerilla battles with the Celts. The Britons had learned by watching their neighbors in Gaul fighting the Romans and realized conventional warfare would mean a swift end; so they at last adopted a new method of fighting and it turned out to be quite successful for over seven years. The man who was heading the resistance was a Welsh Celt name Caratacus. He might of indefinitely kept the Romans at bay head it not been Queen Cartismandua of the Brigantes traitor him and turned him over to the Romans.

Relatively speaking the Romans were content to simply hold onto what they had and get on with commerce with the inhabitants of Britain. For about 20 years the Romans and the Britons coexisted in some semblance of order; especially in Iceni well north of Londinium. However, everything came crashing down around the Romans when the Governor refused to recognized Boudicca as legitimate Queen successor of King Prasutagus. With a small armed force he walked into the Iceni land confiscated their possessions, whipped Boudica for her opposition, and had her daughters gang raped.

The timing was extremely poor for the Governor for the Roman Legends under Suetonius Paulus were way up in Anglesey subduing a revolt lead by the Druids. Boudicca with an army of over 100,000 marched first on Camulodinum and then on Londinium and slaughtered over 80,000 Romans. The surprise ambush nearly wiped out the Roman IX legion. The Celts were now marching straight for Paulus's army of not more than 10,000.

With odds of 10 to 1 it should have been an easy win for the Celts. Yet once again the Celts went at the Romans in their usual mob fashion. Somewhere near the centre of Britain, Paulus picked his a perfect position to line up his small force. They were between two groups of trees so the Britons couldn't out-flank them very easily. Sure enough, the Britons came over the hill in mass and saw the tiny Roman triple line defence and thought this is going to be only too easy. In a mad rush like an enormous tidal wave the Celts crashed down on the Romans, but like so often before they soon found themselves crammed in and no one could swing their swords. The Romans in typical fashion just pushed forward with their swords jabbing at the beleaguered attackers who simply could not move. Within a few hours the Romans rolled over the Britons slaughtering some 80,000. Boudicca fled the field with her daughters and committed suicide. Thus the rebellion came to a crushing end.

Paulus and the Roman Governor were recalled back to Rome and a man named Agricola took over. He was given instructions that the Britons were to be treated fairly and so with a new style of management the unde-cided Celtic stated became client states like the Brigantes who ruled the entire central section of the island. As it was Agricola had an easy time of it of moving Roman conquest all the way up into northern Britain. However, here he ran into three nations that decided to resist any further advancement of the Romans; in 77 AD Agricula was faced with going to war with the combined forces of the Selgovae, the Damoni, and the Caledonians. It came as surprise that the ensuing battle turned into yet another horrific blood bath where phenomenal casualties were incurred by the Celts.

In 78 AD Agricola advanced well into the now Scotland, finding a new and more ferocious enemy: the Picts of whom even to this day almost nothing is known.. The savagery of these people was said to be even worse than that of the Celts. From 78 AD to about 140 AD, fighting the Picts was a never-ending nightmare for the Romans. In frustration the famous 'Hadrian's Wall' was built across what is basically now the southern border of Scotland. There was said over twenty major garrisons stretched along an 80 mile front with 4 legions tied up defending it. Mind you a new foe came onto the scene and Agricola made mention of it to the historian Titus, and that was the Hyberians or Scottis from Ireland. They had come in alliance to the Picts and together were a sure pain in the sides of the Romans. Just as Agricola was going to do something about it he was recalled back to Rome.

Reflection of the Celtic Empire

The Celtic empire got going with Brennus sacking Rome circa 390 BC and right up to 200 BC the Celts were at their peak of power; that's about 190 years of ruling the whole of Europe and part of Eurasia. Then, starting with the Carthaginians taking their land in southern Iberia (Spain) around 210 BC, began the slow decline. The Romans took close to a hundred years to finally take Iberia; mind you the fall of Gaul one has to admit was quick by comparison and then took another 80 years to finally conquor the other ¾'s of Britain. Ireland on the other hand was never taken. As such, one last bastion of the Celtic world survived. It is from this that a major point has to be driven home, and that is the Celts despite how many writers try to make it look that way did not collapse quickly at the hand of Julius Caesar. The fall of Gaul was only one piece of a once massive empire. Had Caesar faced Brennus (I) it may well have been a different story. Brennus, for what little is written about him, was as much a tactician as was Caesar himself plus had a far more massive army at his disposal, and as such there is little doubt he would have easily have rolled over Caesar. To this date he would have been the one to have disappeared from history.

So when you finally tabulate the final numbers the Celtic empire age dwindled at a painfully slow pace. Between Carthage and Rome combined it took them 280 years to finally put an end to the Celtic Twilight. And, remember Briton was not so much as conquered as it was simply occupied and Ireland (Scotland) was allowed to remain Celtic for yet another thousand years before at last the Normans arrived.

CHAPTER 6

The Land of King Arthur

"Uther. You shall be king of all Britain.
For the star and the fiery dragon under it,
Signifies yourself.
And the ray extending to the Gallic coast
Portends you shall have a potent son."

GEOFFREY MONMOUTH

Calling it the land of Arthur establishes two identities. The first one is the time frame; here we are referring definitely to the fifth century for those are well familiar with the Arthur legend. The second of course is the place; the great legend of Arthur took place in Great Britain and nowhere else. Not too many authors that I know talk of this period of the British history in any other context. Generally speaking when it comes to English they tend to identify time through their monarchs. It is from this I have decided to make the same type of reference. As

91

such what is going to follow here are all the events in this time and the people who played a part in it. It is not just going to be about the King Arthur, but more the Celtic influences that had re-emerged in this period.

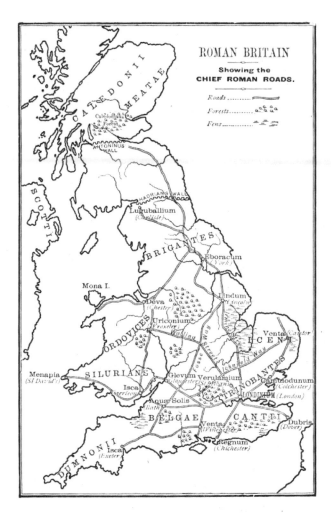

Map of Roman Britain and client kingdoms

Early Briton

Britain, like much of Western Europe was originally inhabited by a people known as the Urnfield people. They came to Britain about 2500 BC. As mentioned earlier many of all the stone monuments on the island were erected in this time period and carried on right up to when the Celts finally arrived. It is very odd that though the Urnfield people had occupied the country for a considerable amount of time very little is known about them. Stonehenge, it has only recently been revealed, was actually a burial ground and not a ceremonial centre as had been the going understanding. Other than that none of the stones have revealed much of who these people were.

Circa 450 BC the first Hallstatt Celtic invasion occurred and this was followed by a La Tène Celtic Invasion c. 300 BC. In it, the names and places did become identifiable and many have survived to this day. In this time the name Britain for example had still not occurred. The Celts had the island divided into three major nations of people. In the south central east part of the island was the LLoegres. In the east central part was the Cymri, and in the north were the Albyne people. Within these three main types of people existed several Celtic-like tribal nations. An example of this is in LLoegres were the Iceni and Belgae nations. In Cymri, just to mention a few, were the Dumoni, Silure and Brigantes. And for the most part in the north were the Picts (Pretani) and some Scotti.

When the Romans came in 43 AD and finally had themselves officially secured in 71 AD of course the island was formally named Britannia. There does not appear to be any information as to how the Romans came to this identity. As for the island it got broken up into what could be described as Roman provinces. In the south coastal region was Britannia Prima, just above it in the central east was Flavia Caesarensis, directly west in the now Wales was Britannia Seconda, and in the north (Northumberland region) was Maxima Caesarensis.

The Roman political purpose was to eradicate as many of the Barbarian tribes as was humanly possible; in Gaul all the Celtic tribes were assimilated out of existence. In Britannia the Iceni, the Brigantes, and the Belgae the Romans managed to also stamp out of existence. However, it was for the first time getting too expensive to fully subjugate all the Celtic nations, thus the Romans allowed what was referred to as "client states" to continue to exist such as the Dumonii, in the now Cornwal, the Silures and the Ordovices in Wales. This move had a huge impact on the island when the Romans finally left in 410 AD. The client states were still fully intact when the legions left and thus with their tuathe size warrior bands were the only ones armed. The Roman citizens who were left behind were unarmed and as such fell prey to the former Celtic tribes in the area.

As the story goes of all the Britannians, the Britannia Secunda region was the most capable of taking over the country and they did: first by Constantine III, then briefly by Aurelius and finally Vortigern. Maybe because of the monastic writing of the time like Nennius and Bede the island's name changed yet again. It was now a simply Britain. However, except for Dumoni new names for the regions started to emerge. Wales for example got broken up into five regions, Dyfed in the south west, Glamorgan on the coastal south, Gwent for most of the central area and Gwyned in the North West corner. In the former Brigante region it became Damoni. Seeing the regions that were fully romanized in the south east it's likely that their names remained in their Roman origins. There is no mention that any new Celtic names were reassigned to this part of the country.

Excluding the Arthur legend, there is next the Anglo Saxon Age that started in c.440 AD and completely took over all of England in 700 AD. It is in this period many of the former Roman identities are eliminated and Saxon ones are put in place of them. For openers the Anglos and the Saxons called the Britons "Welsh." Apparently this was a disrespectful term meaning 'slaves' and over time the name stuck. From here, asthe Saxons slowly made their way across the island, it got broken up into new regions which were more kingdoms then actual provinces. In the east it was the kingdom of East Anglia, in the south were the kingdoms of Kent and Sussex, to the west the Kingdom of Wessex, the central region the kingdom of Mercia and in the north the Anglo Kingdom Northumbria.

Now all this becomes important when trying to comprehend all the nonsense that has resulted from Geoffrey Monmouth's sensational story of King Arthur. The modern day Britain is under the impression King Arthur was a Briton and understandably so. He gets addressed this by Nennius and Tsylio, plus the Cambraie Annals. This in fact is what everybody was prior to the Saxons coming. But as mentioned, over the next 300 or so years the Saxons squeezed what was left of the Britons into Wales and Cornwall. These remaining Britons are now referred to as "Welsh." No longer the dominant race on the island of course, they go by the new designation. It's this that modern Britons are confused about. They don't see the Welsh as former Britons, but simply Welsh as they were named by the Saxons. Therefore, they are under the misconception that King Arthur was of the Britain they know today, not as it actually was. They don't for moment realize that King Arthur was both a Briton and a Welshman (as called by the Saxons at the same time).

You see, Geoffrey Monmouth and later Chretien De Troyes, gave the story of Arthur the 12th century age of chivalry twist of the knights of the round table; the real story is now completely lost to Hollywood.

Trying to figure out the political landscape at the time when King Arthur came onto the scene is to say the least very confusing especially when you have people like Bede and Gildas who because of their extreme religious zealousness simply refer to all the Britons' Kings as "tyrants." As such scholars today simply refuse to connect the dots on who was likely king at the time when certain great events like the Battle of Baedon took place.

When you go into Wales you find the story of King Arthur told matter-of-factly. It t follows the Celtic format that is readily understandable by anyone who understands the Celtic culture. There are no knights of the round table, no holy grail and no sword being pulled out of a stone. King Arthur came to power in the usual Celtic format, first elected as a warrior band leader like Vercingetorix and Boudicca, and once he proved himself was later elected as Ard Ri. The real story is amazingly straight forward.

When the Roman legions left in 410 AD the most Roman-like military establishment still in existence was indeed down in Tintagel Cornwall. Archaeologists have now since proven this Roman city was the most thriving business community in all of Britain. Here was a man name Constantine III, a Roman Briton who immediately took charge of the Country with the largest single military force of the island. He was politically backed by Ambroisus of Wroxeter Gwent. Vortigern up in Glamorgan rightly saw that Constantine was Roman and thus figured this was the chance for the Celtic Britons to at long last retake their country. The Ard-Ri system is where Vortigern had the edge over Constantine. He could amass the support of all the major Celtic nations under one banner and easily over take Constantine, which he did. However, as we know from earlier he screwed up by calling in the Anglo Saxons to help fight the invading Picts and Scotti and was dethroned. For a brief while Briton technically fell under the command again of Roman leadership of Ambrosius. This lasted until 470 AD when Ambrosius died by mysterious means. For about 10 years the Celtic nations in a very loose confederacy continued fighting the Saxons but not having a single leader made things difficult on the battlefield. Silure (Glamorgan) had still the best reputation for producing the best warriors in all of Britain and at the time it was ruled by a King Meurig. He in turn had a well-trained,ambitious son named Arthur who appears to have to have gained the favour of the other tuethe Kings to lead their combine forces against the Saxons. It is true that over a number of years Arthur went on a series of attacks which were all successful which culminated at

Mount Baedon, where the Britons formally crushed the combine forces of the Anglo Saxon armies. From The Saxon Chronicles we learn that the leaders of the Anglo Saxon forces were commanded by King Aelle and Octa for the Angles and King Cerdic for the Saxons.

The real Arthur story as can best be determined

The year 410 AD is a well-known date to most people in the United Kingdom today. This was the year that the Roman Legions finally pulled out of "Britannia." However, research has determined that the year 406 AD was when most of the Roman legions pulled out of the country and what few cohorts remained were withdrawn in 410 AD. As the story goes, Emperor Honorius called for the re-enforcements from the legions in Britannia in 406 AD to Gaul. However, the Legions only made it to the river Rhone where they were ambushed and subsequently slaughtered. Interestingly this event gets a minor note in history as compared to the defeat of the single 9th Legion that was wiped out in Pictland two centuries earlier.

For maybe a decade things were said to be relatively calm. A man named Aurelius Ambrosius took charge of things from Wroxeter in the Welsh province of Powy. Powy is in the northeastern section of the now Wales. Also, he had an ally in Dumonia (Cornwall) who is commonly known as Constantine (III). Between these two men they maintained for a brief while a Romano-Briton still. However, Powy is relatively a small province with limited political power as compared to the province of Glamorgan in southern Wales that had enormous power. Here it so happens a strategic wedding took place between Vortigern and an influential princess Severa. Nenenius is said to be our best source to consult about the full story of how events soon followed after this. After the marriage Vortigern jumped at the chance to grab the power that came with the unification.

Vortigern it seems was fully aware that Britannia was for the most part a patch of Roman Civitates and Celtic Tueth kingdoms. With the withdrawal of the Legions the Roman Officials weren't fools; they knew sticking around simply wasn't safe. As it was Roman villas, towns and major centres like Londinium all slowly began to be abandoned. However, for the Celtic Britons they remained and began occupying the land being abandoned. Certain regions returned their former glory and they were Dumonia (Cornwal), Gwent (Wales), Glamorgan (Wales), Dyfid (Wales), Durotriges and Manua Gododdin (Northumbria). Brigante which took up most of central Britannia was still being recognized as the Roman province Britannia Secunda. Londinium region was retaken by the Trinovants. Wales, as mentioned, was for the most part under Vortigern's control. He saw a unique opportunity by way of the Celtic tradition in becoming the first Ard-Ri prior to the days of the Roman arrival.

From many contemporary historians Vortigern is often seen as a reckless leader who simply seized power and nothing more. However, when you review the earlier chapters on Celtic tradition of electing their leaders you soon realized Vortigern would not have had much success had he started in this direction. Remember the Celts were by nature quick to fight. Further, it has to be noted Vortigern was quite young and the older chiefs would not take kindly to an upstart pushing them around. As it was Vortigern had to use all his political skills to woo the other Chieftains and convince them that it was in their best interest to elect an Ard-Ri soon or be overrun by yet another invader. In this case the menace was the Irish and Picts.

Now coming back to Aurelius Ambrosius a man who was the son of a Roman consul and generally regarded himself as already taken control of Roman Britannia; the activities of Vortigern became as a real annoyance. In fact it's said the two actually physically clashed at one point. The source for most information about this estranged relationship was the monk Gildas. His religious tirades made the details of the events very vague. The bottom line is Aurelius tried with his connection of the Roman Britons and Constantine to counter Vortigern and but in the end failed. It's generally agreed that by 425 AD Vortigern became officially the Ard-Ri of all of "Britons."

The Irish Threat

His name was Niel Ui-Neil, commonly known as "Niel of the Nine Hostages." From the Irish legends and chronicles the young warrior was in nature very similar to that of Alexander the Great. Circa 420 AD he came to power of Hibernia, but at the time the people referred to themselves as Scots. Archaeologists' were able to prove with the invention of the gristmill in 260 AD under King Cormac Mc-Art the Scottish population started to dramatically increase. No sooner did the population began to increase when migration began started in west Caledonia (known as Dal Riada). Apparently because the Picts were being pressured by the Romans they took to the Scots as an ally to help them fight the Romans. The Scot-Pict invasion of 385 AD is the best example of the cooperation between the two peoples.

The west side of Caledonia emerges as an eventual province of Scotland (Ireland) like Leinster, Munster, Connaught, and Ulster. The economy is at its peak in prosperity, when as mentioned, Neil comes to the Tara throne as Ard-Ri of the new, enhanced nation. From examining great documents like saint Patrick's Confession and the Irish Chronicles, it appears that Neil had an enormous fleet of some 400 small war ships. Archaeologists believe the two small Viking ships found just north of Copenhagen (dated to 400 AD) in 1988 were likely the same design of Neil's ships.

Niel no sooner came to power when news of the Roman legions had departed from Britain and the country was vulnerable to attack. The Picts it is said had wasted no time at all and were already systematically ravaging the east coast of Britain. Neil however saw a different opportunity for the Scots and unlike the scavenger Picts his intentions were set on conquest.

According to both Gildas' and Nennius' writings, the Irish scourge started almost immediately after the Romans left; so when Neil came to power time wasn't wasted executing his attack plans. However, we learn that the man was no ordinary Celtic leader. Through a famous poem we find out he has a high level of cleverness.

Four hundred ships and crew
Come unto you Dunaad which is true
Five kings of Scots and one Ard Ri
Without the loss of a single man
Captured all the Picts from earth to sky

The story behind the poem is how Neil got his title "Niall of the Nine Hostages." As can be told by the poem he came to Dal Riada in force; the five kings were the kings of the five Irish provinces. At this time a little more than a third of Caledonia was under Scottish control so it was likely conquering the rest of the country was going to be an enormous fight. However, Neil came up with an ingenious idea, which we will find later was used by Hengist as well: he invited the chiefs of the Picts to a feast. In that invitation the chiefs brought with them their sons and nephews. While the meal was in progress Niall had his men seize the chief's heirs and forced an agreement of lordship over all Caledonia. The chiefs gave in to the demands and in an amazing turn of events the Caledonia became a massive province of Scotland. Hard to believe that in a single move Ireland effectively grew to twice its size.

Niall goes on to conquer parts of Wales, Cornwall, and Brittany. More is explained about him when we get into the history of Ireland. All that needs to be known at this point is that Vortigern had more than his hands full when addressing the Irish scourge.

From acquiring Calidoni the Irish had massed an army of over 30,000. Vortigern didn't even have half that force available to him so he no choice but to call for assistance from the Saxons. More than half of the west coast was under Irish control and in the east the Picts were completely unopposed on the entire coast line. The Saxon Chronicles states that the Picts had stretched their influences down the east coast all the way to the former Roman fortress Camulod. By all accounts it means the Britons were being squeezed into the interior with enemies on two fronts. It gives a whole new perspective to the reason why Vortigern decided to invite the Saxons to help the Britons.

The Saxon Shore

Inviting the Saxons into Britain has been criticized by many historians as Vortigern's downfall decision. Once you start reading up on who the Saxons were it's understandable. The Saxons, the Angles, and the Jutes all principally came from the Denmark region. I have noticed that some writers actually address them as Danish. Like many of the Germanic tribes of this part of Europe, it is true they have a fierce background and this became evident the first time they encountered the Picts. There is no time reference but the impression given is the "Danish" tribes in short order had no difficulty eliminating the Picts from the south east area of Briton. Defeating the Scots, according to the Chronicles, was a little bit more challenging but still manageable. So here's the gist: if the Britons could not handle the Scots and Picts yet the "Danish tribes" could, just exactly what kind of trouble did Vortigern invite to the Island?

According to Bede, Hengist and his son Horas his arrived in Briton in 428 AD, leading the first wave of

Saxons (only). Vortigern offered the two men and their entourages a strip of land down

in Kent plus a form of financial compensation for their services against the Gael hordes. When the Angles arrived next, as mentioned, they had no difficulty driving out the Picts from the lands formerly known as Iceni. Vortigern also invited Cuneda from Gododdin (Northumbria) to drive the Irish out of Gwynned which was done with brutal efficiency. As can be seen Vortigern was coordinating alliances from anywhere he could get them. For the next 10 or so years he managed to achieve relative stability in Britain. There is no doubt this solidified his position as Ard-Ri of the country. However, as we know this was only a brief reprieve.

From the fighting the Saxons came to a quick self realization the Britons were indeed a weak people and thus decided to capitalize off that weekness. They immediately demanded an increased compensation package in both money and lands for their efforts. Vortigern's response was no. Again, according to Bede, things started to get out of hand with Vortigern when trying to keep the peace with the Saxons. He accepted an offered to marry Hengist's daughter, which if you recall Vortigern is already married to Severa of Glamorgan. Historians are still engaged in serious debate as to what happened next. Hengist invited the leading chieftains and Princes of Vortigern's confederacy for a feast that turned into a blood bath. If this event actually took place under Celtic tradition, Vortigern in 437 AD is technically no longer in power. The Saxons immediately broke out in revolt and it is said that Vortimer, Vortigern's son, just manage to contain the rebellion. It would seem the Britons were finally making the grade in their fighting stature with the Saxons. Unfortunately, Vortimer's efforts only lasted for three years when he was forced to leave for Amorica (Brittany).

As for Vortigern, his career was indeed over. It is said he went into exile in the mountains of Snowdonia and from it a new legend surfaced in the Arthurian saga of the famous fight between the white and red dragons. Whatever the circumstance that befell him his removal from power was permanent. According to Gildas, Ambrosius is once again in charge. However, as historians seem to realize if Ambrosius did indeed take command it could only have been in a political sense because basically he was by then a very old man. There is a general consensus that the Welsh kingdoms were effectively in a solid form of a confederacy than ever before. Gildas' interpretation of events is without any dates so we find we have to go to other sources to find out where we are. Luckily from the Saxon Chronicles there is some remedy to this interesting situation. The time is circa 470 AD.

It seems common sense dictated from this point on what would happen next. According to Nennius and Gildas, Ambrosius is confirmed a mature man when Vortigern came to power in 425 AD. Seeing we don't have any precise dates let's say he was in his 30's. That would mean by 480 he would be roughly 85 years old. Clearly at such an age he was far from capable of galloping around the country on horseback to rally the Britons against the Saxons.

The reason for this is to at long last address the possibility that King Arthur was real. As many will know, despite the fact Oxford University in 1964 formally declared he was a genuine person, many still believe he is fictional.

The References of This Time

This time period has been a blur of events because there are so many contemporary historians who have interpreted the story. The reason for this is that our primary people at the time did not write in a straightforward manner as we had become accustomed to from the Roman Titus. The three major sources that modern writers refer to when trying to piece the Dark Age Briton together are Gildas 515 – 570 AD, Nennius, 809 – 850 AD, and Bede 701-755 AD. All three were dedicated monks and it showed in their writing style. All were very free in using the word "tyrant" to describe such major historical figures like Vortigern. As a result what modern historians have been compelled to do is to over ap their accounts to find out who is being talked about. Nennius was the one writer who would actually name a person where the other two would refer to him as unnamed. Take for example the famous battle of Baedon. All three monks confirm this event took place c. 515 AD. Nennius is the only one to actually name King Arthur as a participant in it. As such historians today generally accept that the battle did take place, but are not overly confident that King Arthur was the one who fought in it.

However, of the three monks who wrote their versions of British history it would appear Nennius provides us with the best references to the leading characters in the Arthurian Age. We learn he is the only one to name

Arthur as the King who finally was able to stop the Saxon advance into Britain. As was later learn it was Nennius who Geoffrey Monmouth used as his principal when he wrote his colourful version of the King Arthur. Though Gildas and Bede won't name the Briton who saved the day at Baedon they certainly elude to him.

However, as always the question is, where did Nennius get his source to actually naming Arthur as the man who became King after Ambrosius? It turns out there were two sources. The first one was the Chronicles of Cambria and the second was yet another monk who is well known in Wales but virtually nowhere else. Tsylio is his name; he wrote a historical account of the Kings of Glamorgan and not only does he make reference to King Arthur but also his genealogy in where he came from. Arthur's real father is a man named Meurig and grandfather was Tewdrig. In the Welsh Chronicles this all a simple matter of fact.

As to Arthur being the son of Uther it would appear this was all a fabrication by Geoffrey Monmouth. As if we are surprised by this.

Glamorgan is a small teuth kingdom that was part of Siluria in the very south end of Wales. The story has it the Romans never manage to conquer them and it was Hadrian who through a peace agreement got them to become at last a Client State. As it was Siluria was an independent kingdom that fully manages their own affairs including the recording of their own history.

At last we now know where Geoffrey Monmouth's idea for his King Arthur came from. His book on the *History of the British Kings* is described as being predominantly made up of pure imagination sprinkled with the odd fact. His accounts of Ambrosius Aurelius are one of the amazing points found to be accurate. In such very rare moments he stays true to history. But as many will tell you Geoffrey's version of the British Kings in the Dark Age is simply the work of a vivid imagination.

Arthur Comes to Power

Even without Tsylio's and Nennius' references to Ambrosius's age, it's not hard to figure out when the centrepiece to everything lies in the Battle of Baedon. Most historians have come to the general conclusion this battle did take place, and happened at Bath or somewhere nearby in the time frame of 500-515 AD. The battle of course has two additional sources of authenticity and that being the Saxon and Irish Chronicles. Assuming this is so, and then once more looking at Ambrosius who it is believed by some fought at Baedon, his age can be determined. If Ambrosius was fighting with the young upstart Vortigern in 425 AD as a "mature man" and the battle of Baedon on the least side date occurred of 500 AD, then the difference was 75 years. When you take into account that average age was 40, Ambrosius is beyond a doubt a very old man; hardly someone who would be able to fight a major battle such as Baedon.

In all the references from this point on there are no other persons who are mentioned other than Arthur who lead the Britons in this fight. Thus we are left to believe it may actually be so. Again, Nennius and Tsylio are our two main sources of this final conclusion. The Saxon Chronicles tell us who the main opponents were and they were, Ceredic (Saxon), Aelle, and Octa (Angles). Hengis and Horas had been dead now for about 25 or so years. According to their Chronicles, Ambroisus (not named) had up until 470 AD the Saxon and Angle advances stifled. However, the Chronicle says after this date the Briton Leadership collapsed and so the Saxons went on a major campaign to take advantage of it. The Saxons progressed to take the lands right up to the boarders of Gwent and the Angles completely absorbed what is now called Essex. This advance stopped in 480 AD and the impression of the Chronicles is the Britons were reorganized under a new leadership. Of course once more it is Nennius we rely on to tell us that new leadership is none other than Arthur. However, be aware, he is not a king yet, this is where it is now being recognized he was in the role as a general and from his successes he earns himself the rank of king. Once more this is believable when you start to review the Celtic tradition of their elected leadership process.

The Great Battle

The Battle of Baedon is of course the one resounding event that is fully identified by all the writers of the time, Nennius, Gildas, Bede, the Saxon Chronicles, the Irish Chronicles and the Annals of Cambriae. Where it took place seems likely was just east of Cardiff Wales, the place is exactly as described by Nennius and the name Baedon still survives to this day. The problem with Bath, which most British writers feel is the actually place, is at the time in the 5th century was known as Aqua Sulus. Gildas who was born at the time of the battle would clearly have known the difference between the two places. He makes no mention of it having been at Bath. However, to be fair to both locations, to date archaeologists have yet to find a single piece of evidence that a battle took place at either spot.

As many will know the famous battle was conducted over a period of three days. King Arthur had chosen his ground well on top of a mound. Depending upon who you want to believe Arthur's army was anywhere from 800 to 12,000 cavalry and men. The combined forces of the Angles and Saxons were said to be three times larger than the Britons. From what I have seen of photos of both mounds the grade is fairly steep. A Saxon warrior would indeed be hard pressed to charge up it quickly. Knowing the style of fighting, it's reasonable to believe the invading force

would have suffered serious casualties from the archers alone. But even with this it is believable that the tough nature of the Angles and Saxons they would have persevered. It turns out they charged the hill numerous times over a period of three days. Arthur all this time kept his infantry in tight formation and repelled every onslaught. Finally, on the third day when it was obvious the Saxon forces had seriously dwindled he let loose his cavalry and as we know, won the day.

Whether you believe this or not is actually immaterial. What is incredible is that all sources agree on what happened after the battle, and that is the 30 or so years of peace. Even in the Saxon Chronicles it states there were no more attacks on the Britain until well into 550 AD. So however how the battle was really fought does not matter; its effect definitely stopped the AngloSaxon advance.

In summary, when you go beyond the standard accepted references of Nennius, Bede, and Gildas, plus properly examine the time frame, you have little doubt that a man by the name Arthur came to the forefront in c. 495 AD and was indeed the leading figure of Britain right through to about 530 AD. If he wasn't then who was? British historians somehow have no replacement for Arthur to this very day.

The British Celtic Revival in Decline

With the general consensus Britain had gone into a period of peace of about 30 years; some authors claim a portion of the Saxons people actually returned to Denmark. It would seem at long last the Britons (Welsh as they were referred to by the Saxons) could breathe a sigh of relief. You have to remember to this point in time the Britons had been fighting on a near yearly basis for almost 80 years.

The Saxons were having far greater difficulty taking the country as was originally perceived by Hengist. In fact when you compare it to the Romans in Iberia the end results are even more dismal. The reason for this is the Saxons fought in the similar fashion as the Celtic Britons; long swords and oval shield, one massive mob crashing into the other. As it was the two sides were evenly matched. The individual fighting skills was the only determinant in the results of how the battle turned out. As it was the Britons proved they were more than an equal to their Saxon counterparts.

Then came a very strange natural phenomenon over the land. The weather changed and a five year cold spell swept the land and a strange misty cloud continuously covered the sky. This climate change was the result of a volcanic eruption that occurred in Iceland. Like the 2010 eruption over Great Britain, the misty cloud was actually volcanic ash but its effect was far more wide spread. A massive drought took place and a second major migration of Britons left for Amorica. Amorica was later to become known as Brittany and thus a renewed Celtic nation emerged in the North East corner of Gaul. Amorica is said to have held its own right up to the 8th century.

The migration was noted by the Saxons and in about 560 AD the Saxons simply migrated into the central part of the country. It's in this region many scholars have come to the observation the Saxons really didn't conquer Briton as was stated in most of the literature up about the 1970s but simply migrated in much the same way the Celts did in 400 BC of Gaul. This is so misleading for it will be seen that once the Saxons regained their confidence the fighting erupted once again.

From this point on we are reliant on the Saxon Chronicles and Bede to recount what happened next. A Saxon king named Cewlin started a campaign in much the same way as Ceredic when he came to Briton in 470 AD. Cewlin was convinced he could wear down the Britons in a prolong struggle, however he paid a terrible price for it. The Briton Confederacy comes together again under the King Maelgwn of Gwynned. Which one he is not certain, for like the story of Arthur in legend it turns out there are several versions of this man. The struggle starts in 560 AD and goes on until 616 AD. The Saxons manage to at long last reach the Severn River and divide Dumonia from Wales.

The Britons may have had a better account for themselves had it not been for yet another Anglo King Ethelbert starting a campaign of a similar nature in the north. He was principally fighting the Scots and the Picts. As it was the two major Celtic groups were unable to form a collision in the next three decades of renewed fighting. By 617 AD Northumbria was born and the Scots and Picts were once more relegated behind Hadrian's Wall.

Then starting in 635 AD a bizarre set of events took place. The "Land of the English" – England – which had was broken into 5 major Kingdoms (Mercia, Northumberland, East Anglia, Wessex and Suffix), all erupted into fighting with each other. No doubt the Britons, who were now pushed to the rim of the island, could not have been more delighted with the turn of events. However, staying out of the Saxon Civil war they simply couldn't do. There is one well recorded event c, 645 AD where Cadwellyn of Wales decides to join forces with the Mercians against Ethilfrith of Northumbria and this turns into a disaster. Wales is suddenly vulnerable to be also consumed by the Saxons had it not been Ethilfrith paid an awful price in lives and could not pursue his victory. Once again the reader has to be reminded when the armies of this period fought slaughter was usually the end result. If you won any given battle chances are you often were left with maybe a quarter of your original force. The days of sweeping lopsided victories the Romans enjoyed during the 1st century were over.

The bloodshed is said to have at long last petered out in the start of the 700's. The now six Saxon nations long last decided to develop their own kingdoms. It was claimed of the Saxon Nations Mercia had become the most affluent under King Offa. He was one of the first Saxon Kings to mint coin currency in the land. Judging by the design of the coin he was a young, clean shaven man. Clearly he was a person with modern and advanced ideas to finally make the Saxons a nation respected by their counterparts on the mainland. It was under his ruler ship the famous Offa Dyke was built nearly the full length of Wales. So now Wales was in the same predicament that the Picts endured under the Romans' Hadrian's Wall. However, it does not seem the Welsh minded it because it meant the Saxons had at long last gone on the defensive.

Unfortunately c. 750 AD fighting once more erupted now in Dumonia. The Kingdom of Wessex made one last attempt to take over the Britons in this region and with Domonia (Northumbria) so reduced in size their strength did not hold out. As it was after over 1350 years of independence the Celtic identity was finally snuffed out.

If the other Saxon Kingdoms were thinking along the same lines as Wales and Scotland they were distracted with a problem that took them quite by surprise. The problem was the emergence of Christianity. By 700 AD as the cultural revolution of the Anglo Saxons began to take; each of the Saxon Kings became Christian and allowed the two main churches to thrive in their respective kingdoms. In Northumberland and most of Mercia it was the Celtic Christian church that took hold. In Wessex, Kent, and Suffex the Roman Christian church started by Saint Augustine took over. The various kings welcomed the religions for they felt it gave divine elements to their rule. The warrior mentality of the Anglo Saxons was now evolving to what was later to be called a feudal Lord system.

The problem that came was the taxing the people. Up until now the average Saxon was accustomed to paying one tax and that was to the King. When the various churches started to take hold the people were now finding themselves paying two taxes, one to the king and the other to the church. We can still see the evidence today of the results of this new system. Lindisfarne, Jarrow, Canterbury, Iona, and Glastonbury all became great monastic churches of enormous wealth which became known to the whole of Europe, including the Vikings.

Sure enough c. 798 AD the Saxon world that so briefly in its history had enjoyed a relatively degree of a good lifestyle found themselves in the same predicament as the Celtic Britons had endure for centuries before and that was invasion. The Norseman Vikings as we know struck in the north first, sacking Iona and Lindisfarne first, and when this was found to be too easy in the next decade they came in force and pretty well conquered the whole of Northumbria.

The southern regions were not to be spared either. In this part of the country they were attacked by the Dane Vikings and East Anglia soon disappeared as a result. For a brief while they were able to halt the invading marauders with the appearance of the famed Alfred the Great. However, that didn't last long; by 1300 all of England except Wales and Scotland were conquered and King Cnut of Daneland sat on an overall English throne. You might say he was the very first English King so to speak.

The reason the Welsh particularly survived this era of pillage was they welcomed the Vikings as liberators and joined them in their attacks on the Anglo Saxons. Wales manage to continue as the last Brythonic Celtic nation in Briton until at last King Edward I in 1200 AD extinguished them as well. Scotland managed to hold out out until 1700 when they voted themselves out of existence in the infamous Act of Union with Great Britain. Thus at last the Celtic world in Britain came to its close.

CHAPTER 7

Ireland – Last Celtic Bastion

Be they kings, poets or farmers
They are a people of great worth.
They keep the company with angels,
And bring a bit of heaven to earth. (Unknown)

I am going to end my Celtic story here for it seems to me what happens later in Medieval Europe all stems from the developments that happened in Ireland. It may sound rather bizarre but when you carefully look into it its actually quite true. An excellent book that goes into great detail on this point is Thomas Cahill's *How the Irish Saved Civilization*.

All of Europe was fully submerged in the Dark Ages. The intellectual light of Rome was being ripped apart by the various scavenger nations across the land like the Visigoths, Vandals, Burgundians, and Franks. The only nation that was held intact was of course Ireland.

Its economy was bustling and its population was dramatically growing with the invention of the gristmill. It comes as no surprise that Ireland took full advantage of this era to enter onto the world stage as a new cultural and political influence. In this last chapter I will cover the two major events that are the most significant of this time period. The first one is that Ireland emerged as a physical empire and actually came close to conquering all of England. The second one is one which Ireland is definitely more noted for and that is monastic empire. This religious empire is the one that came unbelievable close to ousting the Roman Catholic Church. It was at the Synod of Whitby in 664 AD the Catholic Church was in the nick of time finally able to arrest the massive expansion of the Celtic Christian Church. Here now is the final story of the Celtic people.

Ireland. The Romans called it Hibernia. Up until 400 AD they referred to themselves as Scotti. This is very different from what was the situation in the rest of the Celtic empire. As we know by now in all the other places throughout Europe the Celts only knew themselves by the name of their tribes, not as a united continental nation.

Hibernia was originally settled by the Hallstatt Celts from Iberia (Spain) c. 350 BC. The original people they displaced or intermarried with were the Urnfield people, who had settled the land about 2500 BC and as was so typical of everywhere else built massive stone monuments like at Newgrange. Similarly the modern the Irish tourist board would have you believe they were built by the Celts as well. You have to admit with all the Celtic revival going on it does make for good tourist dollars.

According to Irish folklore, and trust me this country has lots of it, the country was invaded four times. Archaeological research shows, however, if the Urnfield people actually invaded the island the most the count would be is twice. Why this small and insignificant point is crucial to know is so that you have a basis of understanding about the Celtic peoples' minds and their very creative imaginations. What is universally accepted is that the Irish, because they were not conquered by the Romans, were able to preserve for us today the "mind" of the Celtic civilization. Had Rome successfully conquered Hibernia we would likely have been dependent on the writings of Julius Caesar to know what was going on in the Celtic society. Much of what he wrote on the Celts, he could only compare to what was understood by the Roman society, especially when it came to the Celtic gods. For example, the god Lugh: Caesar had him compared to the Roman God Mercury. When you examine the two gods in their native environments you soon realize the two are not similar at all. To this we give enormous thanks from a historical perspective that the Irish survived the Romans.

From the Irish folklore that includes imaginary invasions, it would seem the Celtic mind was simply silly and ridiculous and thus our modern rational minds automatically thinks this subject is pointless to bother with. However, when we go back to the Battle of Telamon c. 224 BC, without knowing the Celtic mind, this whole battle becomes absolute bizarre. Who in their *right mind* would go into battle completely nude and in many cases not even carrying a shield to protect themselves? Only when you start to get into the thinking of the Celts does this start to make sense. For historians the reason *why* plays a huge factor in trying to understand the way in which an event unfolded. One of the greatest examples to this line thinking is: why on earth did Napoleon ever want to leave Moscow in the dead of winter when he must have known his army would never survive it?

Now that we have some premise for the importance of the Celtic mind we can continue on to what the Irish were able to reveal to us on this subject.

Ireland was at the time of the Christian monks, c. 500 AD, still very much a Celtic nation in the full sense of the word. As such they were able to see firsthand and record the bahaviour in its pure form. Unlike Julius Caesar they did not have a political agenda to play with or any of the Roman gods to make comparisons with either. As such they recorded exactly what they witnessed in its purest form. Saint Finnian c. 600 AD is, so far, our earliest source of the pure Celtic world. It is said he got his first experience recording down what was told to him by the King of Ulster. Saint Finnian must have thought he was in for a long night when one of the very first things the King told him he was a descendent of the Fomorians. Formorians are a fictional people who are said to once inhabit the land centuries before the Gaels (Celt) arrived.

With this first writing we came to later have some of the most incredible stories that give us today an amazing insight into the race. The greatest of the stories recorded is the legendary story "Tain Bo Cuilgne" (The Cattle Raid of Cooley). Then there is the story of Deirdre, followed by Finn Mac Cumhail (Finn McCool). The famous Queen Madb (Queen Maeve) and the Red Branch of Ulster;

finally the Lienster Circle and Ossin, just to mention only a very few examples.

What is found in all these great legends is the incredible imagination of the gods, witches, and Druids and how they interplayed with each other. It comes as no surprise that from these writings how we today comprehend the magical world of King Arthur written by Geoffrey Monmouth and Chretien De Troye.

When you look back at the suicidal mentality that happened at Battle of Telamon you now comprehend the Celts honestly believed that magic was real. *The Romans could never truly kill them.*

Again, it has to be remembered these stories were taken directly by the monks from the original sources, unlike the famed Welsh legends of Mabigonia. Mabigonia was written in the middle of the 11th century and it's for the most part an "interpretative" version of the original legends, put together by Lady Guest.

Getting back to the subject of archaeology, there are very few physical ancient finds in Ireland. As we now know Celts were not ones for building very much out of stone and because of the Druids did not permit anyone to write anything down either; everything was dependant on oral traditions. However in 1985 and 1995 this all changed. There was a huge breakthrough on this subject as result of straightforward upgrading work. In Shannon Bay a massive dredging project took place and from it was uncovered an enormous amount of gold brooches, torcs, and wrist bands. Ireland was also at the time doing some major road renovations on the east coast from Dublin to Wexford when over 80 Celtics burials were uncovered. This amazing discovery was for the first time the archaeologists could now put some fundament time lines to the history of the country.

From the jewelry they were able to confirm the Irish Celt was indeed for the most part Hallstatt. Some La Tène artifacts were found but it is likely this was the results of trade more than from actual cultural existence. In the burials along the east coast was found Roman artifacts to confirm much of the stories about King Cormac Mc Art, in 260 AD, having commerce with Roman Britannia. Of course when the Gaelic language was examined, it too was found to be of Goedilic origins. Next came the discovery of the Ogham stones, origins c. 300 AD. These stones were found throughout the whole of Ireland and it was deemed that the Irish are the originators of this form of writing. This becomes to be a very important point when we start to again look at the Irish migration and conquests into Britain. Thus by the end of 1995 historians were at last able to confirm a number of truths about the mysterious country.

The premises around the Ogham writing is the Druids became aware of Roman writing and as such they developed their own.

So now putting it all together, Ireland around 100 AD was composed of four major tribes. In the North West, now the province of Ulster, were the "Ui Neils." In county Antrim were the "Ulaids." In Leinster the dominant tribe was the "Ui Dunlaigne." In Munster the dominant tribe was "Eogananacht Aine" and in Connaught it was the "Ui Fiachrach." Historians discovering this have recently called into question the names the Romans addressed the Celtic Tribes on the main continent. Whether you speak Goedilic or Brothonic Gaelic the way the words are pronounced is for the most part very difficult and often from the back of the throat. There is no doubt that Romans dismissing the Celts as simple barbarians and would not even attempt to pronounce the names correctly. Thus there is now discussion as to what real names of the various tribes may actually have been.

In legend and later in actual history it was found the Ui Neil was the overall ruling tribe on the island for the longest period of time. The capital Tara is said did not come into existence until the middle of the 2nd century and therefore it is no surprise the Ui Neil ruled as the Ard Ri for most of its history. "Niall-of-the-Nine-Hostages" (Ui Neil) is both in legend and archaeological evidence was indeed one of the truly greats kings to exist. His reign was c. 440 – 453 AD. Historians have no difficulty now saying it was one of his raids that Saint Patrick as a boy was taken as prisoner to Ireland and sold to a farmer up in Ulaid territory. King Cormac Mc Art was another great name. It is now firmly believed in his time period of 260 AD that great legend of Finn McCool existed. Further, archaeology has confirmed he was the king who introduced the gristmill to the country. This made an enormous change in the population growth. Finally there is King Brian Boru in 1100 AD. He of course is not found so much in legend as he is in straight history. His great accomplishment on the little island was at long last subjugating the Vikings.

The Irish Empire in the 4th Century

Now for the great Scot invasion of the land of the Picts and how Ireland eventually became an empire in its own right. It's a remarkable story that was noted by both in Bede's and Gilda's writings. The stage was set when the Romans had pulled out of Britain and the city of Rome had been sacked by the Visigoths. As mentioned in c. 440 AD the young energetic Niall of the Ui Neil Clan took to the throne at Tara. With a strong economy and an enormous military he felt the time was right for Scotland (Ireland) to make history. Mind you being an unusually young ruler he had to first deal with subduing the provincial kings. They did not take kindly to a youth being Ard-Ri. A number of fierce battles took place where Nial quickly proved he was a brilliant commander of men. Once Ireland was a solid unified nation he now focused on the weakened Briton and other parts of Europe that the Romans had since withdrawn from, such as Brittany.

Niall's first big move was to Calidoni (now Scotland, as named by the Romans), seeing as already about a third of the land was already in Scottish hands. This was because the dominant Celtic tribe closest to Hadrian's Wall was the Calidoni tribe. However, so typical of Roman ignorance, there were two other major tribes in existence along with the Calidoni, and they were the Votadani who occupied much of the northwest part of the country and their capital was Dun Eidin (Edinburgh), and the Damnoni tribe that occupied the lands just west of the Calidoni and straddled down into Northumbria. Irish historians believe there was in the 2nd century a major uprising between Eoganacht Aine (Munster) and the Ui Neils (Ulster). In the turmoil the Ulaids were the first to migrate to Calidonii. Yet according to Irish historians it is said the real reason was that a plague broke out and a man by the name Fergus Mor Mac Eirc took a band of Irish people and simply migrated to Calidoni. The British understanding is that they were invited to help fight the Romans. However, it may be more of a case the Picts allowed the "Scots" to stay only if they'd join in their cause. The alliance continued from 100 to 400 AD. The west coast of Scotland we know today was Scotti and the east side was Pict. The Scotti part of the land was known as Dal Riata. "Scotland," as we know it today, became a whole nation at the hand of Kenneth Mc Alpine c. 834.

Once again we have to have brief stop at this point to clarify who the Picts were. The name Picts is what the Romans addressed them by. Unfortunately over the centuries this name stuck. The reason is these "Celts" were into blue body tattooing. Why I say they were Celts when the general understanding is they are a mystery cultural is as a result of findings from the recent studies that have been completed just this decade. The Picts it turns out are Godilic Celts and yes they first came to the northern Briton circa 450 BC. It has also been revealed, like the Scots, they too had a name for their nation of people. They called themselves the people of Pretani. Archaeology confirmed this point for like Ireland there is no written records except Bede's to go on. The evidence shows they lived in similar round homes like other Celts, wore plaid clothing, and their weapons were also of similar designs of the Halstatt period. Like the Irish they had fostering as common practice and taking hostages to secure political alliances was also an established tradition. This last point becomes a key factor to note when at last Nial of the Nine Hostages arrives c. 438 AD.

Nial set off in a fleet of some 400 hundred fast-sailing Viking designed ships for Calidoni. Never in their occupation of Britain did the Romans control the Irish Sea. As such the Sea was indeed completely in Scotti hands. Archaeologists believe each ship could hold about 40 or so men, this would mean at any given time Niall had an army of around 16,000. When Saint Patrick says in his Confession that more than a thousand slaves were taken in his Romano Briton community it's not hard to believe looking at the size of the Scot forces.

The story of how Niall got his nick name, Niall-of-the-Nine Hostages, actually starts in Calidoni. When the Scotti army lands everyone is poised for a bloody campaign, for after all the Picts were both equal in size and equal in fighting ability. As the *legend* goes the combined forces of the Picts appeared on the boarders of Dal Riada and sure enough the potential battle was going to be nothing short of brutal. Nial's quick wit upon seeing the Picts saved the day.

He sent an envoy to meet with the Clan Chiefdoms and their immediate relations for a preliminary parlay if you will. Sure enough the Picts indulge Niall in his request and the leaders meet only to discuss the reason Niall has brought an army to Calidoni. No sooner did they meet when out of nowhere Niall's soldiers seized the Chiefdom's siblings and made them his hostages. Using Celtic tradition of procuring loyalty Niall set the terms to the kings they were to now swear loyalty to Scotland (Ireland) otherwise he would slay their family members. The three major leaders agreed and without so much a single drop of blood, all of Pretani-land became a province of the Scotti. This event is even commented on in the writings of Saint Patrick. Thus the so called legend does have credence. However, what really happened does not matter; it was a fact that Ireland suddenly doubled in size and now was in an amazing position to actually having the potential of conquering Britain. Nial's military forces had doubled in size as well. By way of Celtic rules of loyalty Niall's forces were now around 32,000 men. Vortigern, to counter the Scots, at best had the armies of about five confederate kingdoms and if we are to say they are similar in structure to the Scots he would likely have an army of not more than 15,000. If this was the situation, then it becomes all the more clear why he called upon the Saxons for help.

With Pretani secured Niall turned his attention to Wales in 440 AD. Wales was where the balk of Vortigern's army was stationed and it turns out Niall did not properly anticipate this. As it was when his army landed in Anglesey (northwest Wales) he was met with stiff resistance. Through Welsh history, we are told that Niall fought a prolonged campaign to what is now known as Gwenyd. He did eventually conquer it. For the record the Celtic tribe he fought against was known as the Ordovices. Nial had better luck when he moved onto the south west end of Wales and quickly took the land of the Dematae or as it came to be later known, Dyfed. Dyfed remained in Irish hands well into the 7th century.

There is one last account of the Irish invading Britannia by force and that is said to have happened near where the City of Chester now exists, circa 463 AD. The size of the invasion force was never recorded yet it was said to be massive. Apparently the Britons had to call upon assistance from all regions of the land including

Northumbria to repel the invaders. In a vicious battle the Britons managed to force the Irish to withdraw and that was said to be the last invasion of the country. Causalities are claimed to have been over 15,000.

Next came Cornwall, which was another former Roman Client Kingdom of the Domoni. It's largely believed, seeing there is no evidence of conflict, either in Cornish legend or in general British history, Nial must have used the same tactic against the Domoni as he did with the Picts. The Ogham stones carvings indicate to today proof of the Irish presence. There was said to be hundreds all around the peninsula. Some Academics claim these stones came into existence during the Christian period c. 500 AD. However, C14 testing puts them back much further, thus giving credibility the Irish story was indeed here from the time of Niall.

Nial though he was having remarkable success, his men were beginning to tire of the prolonged wars and dissension was starting to appear. Yet the Scots followed him now into Veneti land (Brittany) of Gaul. Once more the Veneti were also tricked into providing hostages and Nial decided he would take his chances and venture deeper into more pronounced territory of the Romans. There is mention of Nial running into Romans about a hundred miles south on the River Loire and later he ran into the Moroni Celts. Once more Niall secured his "ninth" hostage but it is at a cost of his own life. A man by the name of Eochaidh of Ui Dunlaigne tribe of Leinster assassinated him. The circumstances are somewhat the same as Alexander the Great; mind you Alexander was able to escape the threat of his mutineers. Once more the

Ogham stones are again the evidence archaeologist are using as claim proof of the Irish "invasion."

The Great Legend of Niall

By British historians' accounts, the middle of the 5th century is well recognized as a time when Britain was in a mess. Irish raids were going unchecked all down the west coast of the island and Pict raids were equally doing the same amount down the east coast. Vortigern who had just become the first Ard-Ri of Briton since pre-Roman days only had an available military force primarily from the Welsh states. Central Briton which was principally Roman had no defence; they relied on the legions for protection that are now all gone. When we think of raids we naturally think along the lines of the Vikings, a band of marauders making a quick attack and as quickly as they came they were gone. In this regard it makes no sense that the state be under any threat of being overrun. If this was the situation in Britain at the time of King Vortigern it does not make any sense why he would go to the Saxons for help against the Irish. Clearly the Irish were just a nuisance more than anything. However, as mentioned, through the eyes of the British historians the threat was definitely far more than just coastal raids; so the questionis just how much more serious was it" British history books don't clearly state it, so you are left with no choice but go to the Irish authorities to see if they can explain it. As it turns out the desperation of the Britons was the fact far more serious than British writers have led us to believe. You would hate to think that petty politics between the Irish and the British today is what kept piece of history from being known.

The evidence to this point is in the archaeology. The art of Ogham is clearly given to the Irish and no one else. According to Irish historians in all the locations where it is said Niall of the Nine Hostages had conquered are found Ogham stones. These are not to be confused with the Christian ones that started coming into light in the 6th century. The Christian stones are readily recognized with having both Latin and Ogham writing on them at the same time. Archaeologists have confirmed that the distinct Druid Oghams are found in Brittany, western Scotland, Anglesey, Dyfed and southern Cornwall. This is one source of confirmation of Nial's actual conquest success and of course the other is as mentioned Bede's and Gildas' writings at the time.

King Loegaire, nephew of Niall, came to the Thrown of Tara next in 461 AD. When you read about him you get a sense that Ireland was going through its own version of the War of the Roses. However, most of the fighting was between Leinster and Tara. In the writings done about Saint Patrick we learn Loegaire was fully aware that Ireland was a massive empire like it had never been before; keeping it together was his main focus.

It is likely under his rule was when all the Ogham stones started to be erected in all the different locations that were now in Irish control. Loegaire proved to be a solid administrator, balancing conflict with holding everything together. When Saint Patrick arrived, as much as Loegaire was annoyed with his presence he figured it would be wise not to make a scene especially with everything else that was going on. When we swing back into

Britain we find the Saxons had started their campaign against the Picts and were being successful. After this, Gwenyd falls to a Welsh attack which was definitely well documented in Welsh history for they were quite proud of this accomplishment. Under pressure from the Picts, Loegaire sent a force to alleviate the Saxon incursion. It was not described the size of the force that landed at the now city of Chester, but historians say a combined army of both Britons and Saxons to repel the Irish attack in 465 AD. Lastly when we go into the stories around King Mark in Domoni and his ongoing battles with the Irish attackers here too you get a real sense of the massive size of the Irish forces. When going over all these well-documented British, Welsh, and even Saxon records of Irish strength it clearly confirms that what is said about Nial-of-the-Nine-Hostages has more than enough credence.

Celtic Legends and Facts

Matching the stories and legends in general, despite what anyone says there are many confirmations on the Celtic society. It would appear Caesar's observation that the Druids wielded immense authority was well founded. However, the political authority to motivate the tribes into war was not entirely true. Looking at the Bo Tan, Queen Medb was completely on her own when she decided to invade Ulster. All she wanted from her Druid was to know if she was going to win the war. As for Boudicca, there is no evidence she ever consulted a Druid when decide to rebel against the Romans. Finally there was Vercingetorix and his rebellion in Gaul; again, no consultation with any Druid is evidenced. It would seem for the most part Druids operated principally in an advisory and ceremonial capacity and ceremony much the same as priests we in the medieval age. However, Druids did have an influential presence over the political and religious aspects of Celtic society.

The Druid hierarchy was confirmed through the various legends, plus we get for the first time a taste of how the oral system works amongst the Druids. The first level of a Druid was a Bard. The extraordinary number of poems he had to learn to get to the next level is incredible. If the writings by Brian Boru are any indication, the very minimum a Bard had to know was well over 200 poems. The poems that are found in the Tan Bo have in many cases over a dozen verses in it. Next of course was the Brehon (lawyer/judge). From the writings of the monks there is today an actual example of the legal system that existed in Celtic Ireland. Everything was measured in threes. You have three opportunities to make things right and of course payment for penalties were assessed in threes as well. As an example, causing personal injury to someone may have cost you three cows.

Celtic women, again seen in the Tan Bo as well as in the Leinster Circle, clearly had far more freedom then their female Roman counterparts. A Celtic woman had the freedom to chose who she wanted to marry. She could become a Druid or even a Queen if the opportunity allowed. Lastly, she was just as aggressive in her sexual conduct as her male counterpart and this is not only recorded in Irish legend but by the writings of Saint Paul and numerous Irish monks. Marriage was not a sacred event as it was in the Christian world, except in the case of a King or Queen. A woman could easily divorce her mate in the presence of a Brehon by simply saying she divorced him three times and it was done. In the case of Ard-Ri this was different and in both Ireland and in Denmark there is evidence that being a ruler could be a very dangerous decision. A potential ruler was baptized in the blood of a white horse standing nude in a large cauldron. He had to recite a minimum of nine poems and then have sex with nine other rulers who could be Druidresses as well. If in his reign he was found unfit for the job in many examples his career often ended in strangulation. Finally, if a woman wanted to take part as warrior in battle there was nothing stopping her. There is enough evidence of this last point not only Celtic legend but eye witnesses such as Titus.

Saint Patrick kicks it off

Before we can get into the religious phenomenon that broke out in Ireland and had its influence stretch all the way to the Alpines of Italy, we have talk of whom or what the impetus was. In this case it was Saint Patrick.

As I am pretty sure from the annual Saint Patrick's Day that is celebrated right around the world it will basically be known universally that Patrick had his beginning as a slave. There is continued debate over where he was abducted, whether it was near Cardiff in Wales or up near the wall of Hadrian. I personally think it was up near Hadrian's Wall simply because I could see Nial Ui Neil sailing his massive navy up the Severn where the area is heavily populated and well-armed with the soldiers of Silure. He surely would have run into a fight. Hadrian's Wall on the other hand had been stripped of all its defenses 20 years earlier by the Romans and thus an easy target to pillage to whatever extent the Scots wanted. When you read Saint Patrick's Confession he (Nial) clearly states they took thousands into captivity with complete ease.

Saint Patrick was taken to what is now called Down Patrick which is basically across the bay from the Hadrian's Wall and sold to a tuath lord up in Ulaid (Antrim) territory. For the next six years he worked as a slave tending to sheep; it was during this period of hardship that he seriously embraced religion as the mostly likely means to his own survival. Whether it was real or not, after those brutal six years as slave he had a vision from which he was told its time to go home.

If what he wrote was true it does seem remarkable how things unfolded. Rather than simply go to the closest port that was maybe 40 or so miles to Down Patrick, he travelled the full length of the Irish east coast down to Wexford to get on a ship with a dog trader.

Only recently has it been finally confirmed Saint Patrick did not return to his native Britain but instead went to Gaul. If we are the take the Welsh argument that Saint Patrick was from Wales we know it would have been a sailing of a few hours at best. Had he returned to the Hadrian's Wall region that the voyage would maybe one day at the most. As it turns out he was on the ship for over three days of very turbulent waters. Accounts of this journey claim that he was sailing off the coast of Normandy for even today these waters are still rough to sail in even on the mildest days.

When they landed the crew joined Patrick to find his "father's" place. Patrick as we know did not have any money so he promised the merchant he would be paid once he got home. However, it took them over 30 days to do so through terrain which was basically as a massive uninhabited waste land. Western Britain c. 430 AD was still heavily populated and was for the most part secured by Vortigern; plus the Saxons had yet to arrive. Gaul on the other hand was a completely different story. The land was had been ransacked by the Visigoth, the Vandals, and finally the Franks. It is very plausible in this situation that Saint Patrick and the seamen were crossing Gaul. In what direction it still unknown.

However, we find in the next entry of his Confession that Patrick was now in the south of Gaul on the Mediterranean taking his first instruction to becoming a priest. Thus it is natural to think him when he was traveling with the seamen he had traveled south and may have known of a monastery there from his father who was Deacon. Patrick as history has shown only stayed a year when he moved up to a monastery in Auxeres in northern Gaul; there he stayed for about 12 years when again he has a vision in which he was told to return to the land of his captivity.

Dates on his return would put him in around 460 AD, yet oddly enough the definitive date is still a massive debate. Nevertheless we know it was sometime in this period he did return to Hibernia as a bishop. What the world looked like at the time is that Rome had been ransacked by the Visigoths, and Gaul was now for the most part under Frank rule. Britain was in turmoil for the Saxons were now in a state of rebellion. Vortigern was slowly losing his grip on power. In Ireland Nial was now dead and his son Loegaire (Ui Neil) was now the Ard-Ri.

(New promote) Bishop Patrick was not the first missionary to Ireland as some would believe. In the south end of the country near the now city of Cork a small mission in Armore under a Saint Declen had been thriving for years. As such it is believed Bishop Patrick was under instructions to build on what was there. However, his arrival was not at good time. The new set up Irish empire was already in a state of uncertainty. The death of Niall Ui Neil at the hands of an assassin from Leinster "Ui Dunlaigne" naturally developed into a civil war. And actually he did attack Leinster at one point which turned into a fiasco where he found himself getting captured.

King Loegaire was a big, quiet, and a suspicious man who was fully aware, in these uncertain times, that he was in danger of being the next to go under an assassin's knife, so he had to be careful. Perhaps this was just the ideal environment for Bishop Patrick to spread the Christian faith in Ireland. According to his Confession he had very little difficulty traveling the country. He was particularly welcomed in both Munster and in Connaught and the claims are he baptized both provincial kings.

He doesn't say it, but historians are confident he knew that Ulster was where the real power of the country lay and it was there that he built the primary cathedral on the island in what now known as Armagh.

After some 30 years of enormous success it is odd to discover that Bishop Patrick actually had amassed a considerable amount of jealousy in his own hierarchy back in Britain. Maybe it was because by comparison others had nowhere near the success as he did. In those days it would appear Christianity had for the most part only took root in Cymry Wales and virtually nowhere else. As such a conspiracy seems to have developed that almost cost Saint Patrick his life.

Today this area is known as Strathclide, Scotland and it is situated in south central part of the country next to the Hadrian's Wall. Here was a small land-locked tuath kingdom about the size of Glamorgan ruled by as many viewed a very clever, well-educated monarch. His name was Caraticus. By the description of him he was a Romano Briton who deserted the Roman legions when they were pulling out and set up a unique petty kingdom where half of his subjects were Scots and half were Picts. To everyone around, this was an amazing feat, for Picts and Scots would rather slice each other's throats than to admit they could get along with each other.

The Ard Ri Loegaire was aware of Caraticus and as such called him in to his confidence. To a modern day investigator this part of the story would be indeed very intriguing to follow, for how a land does locked lord end up having the entire Irish navy at his disposal, and further, the ability toattack a colony within the Kingdom? Yes, the whole thing does seem just a little suspicious, for this is what happened next.

The story goes that a retinue of high church officials visited Caraticus' garrison. It can only be surmised that they wanted to pass on their dismay with Patrick's mission; and maybe Caraticus passed this on to Loegaire. Again, it is not known what really happened. All we do know is Caraticus was suddenly in possession of the enormous Irish fleet of some 400 ships and went sailing for Down Patrick.

Patrick, according to the legends of Oisin, was just coming home from a mission in Leinster when at a distance he could see that his home colony of Down Patrick was in flames. When he arrived everyone was gone and off on the high seas Caraticus's ship could be seen sailing away. It is said there was over 2,000 converted Irish Christians and they were all taken into captivity back in Strathclide to be sold as slaves.

Bishop Patrick wrote a rather lengthy, innocuous letter to be read to Caraticus demanding for his people to be returned. Caraticus oddly enough allowed the letter to be fully read in his court by one of Patrick's monks. When it was finished Caraticus made no response to it but did allow the monk to return back to Ireland and today you can read the letter in the Book of Ulster.

A few years after this Bishop Patrick died and left behind a nation that was now virtually all Christian. Scholars feel his success was based on two things. First, he seemed to be clever enough to know the only people on the island that had any ability of education were the local Druids. As such he ordained them as Bishops. They already had the respect of the community so there was not going to be much opposition here to the new religion. The second was an old standard trait of the Christian faith and that was good old charity. To the Scots, having a religion that was for the first time compassionate was a whole new experience. Up to this point in time their religion had been all about bravery and war, and perhaps after so many centuries of bloodshed they simply grown tired of it. As it was Scotland (soon to evolve into Ireland) was in now in a new enlightened age.

The birth of the Celtic Christian Church

The common belief that the Celtic Christian church was entirely Irish is not true at all. Apparently the driving force behind the new religion actually came from Briton, from a man by the name of Saint Enda. He had a monastic mission up in Dal Raida and apparently it was quite influential over everyone nearby. From this centre came a monk Saint Iscanius who traveled to Admare (Scotland) and expanded Saint Declan's monastery. Then of course he went on to have other monasteries established in both Munster and Leinster (Ireland). This was going on in 460 AD when Saint Patrick was still very much around doing his mission in the north end of the country. However, the monastic movement at this time was still in its infancy. It was not until late 480 AD when for unknown reasons the monastic movement suddenly took off.

Some say the movement was given an added boost from Saint David in Dyfed Wales. Like Saint Enda he too had made an impact on the people and soon there were missionaries from his centre also traveling to Ireland to expand a very different version of Christian practices: monasticism.

In the next 39 years the monastic movement swept the whole of Ireland and the Romano Christian Church set up by Saint Patrick was soon overshadowed. Armagh remained the holy seat of the country but delegated any authority over its congregation to the local abbots of the various monasteries.

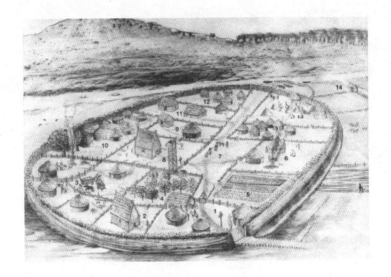

Typical Irish Monastery set up illustration

By the middle of the 6th century Ireland had over a dozen major monastic cloisters across the land. On the borders of Connaught was Clonmacnose established by Saint Cieran. Saint Brendan had set a monastery of Clonfert. Saint Stephen had a serious monastic centre at Glendalough in the north of Leinster. In Kerry and later Iona set up by Saint Colum Cille and again in Leinster was the reknown Kildare Monastery set up by Saint Brigitte.

The Celtic monastic movement took off like wildfire and soon people from all over Europe were coming to the centres across Ireland and Scotland. The monastic movement found its popularity again for very similar reasons as the Christian movement Saint Patrick started: education, following the rules of simple charity, was free to anyone who came. In the Roman Catholic system education was primarily for the well-to-do and came at a cost. Further, the political climate was perfect as well. By the time Patrick had died Europe was completely consumed by the eastern hordes. Gaul alone had been raked over by the Visigoths, Vandals, and finally the Franks. Nearly all traces of the enlightened age of Rome were gone. Pockets of the Catholic Church were spotted here and there in a way in monastic setting, but this was more for protection than an actual community as it was in Ireland. Those who were escaping the barbarian onslaught brought to Ireland their books and thus added enormously to the educational institution of the various monasteries.

When you consider that anything written was forbidden under the laws around the Druids for centuries; to suddenly now have access to the written word was a source of enormous wonder. Reading books, collecting books, and hand writing them was an amazing fascination of all the monks. As we know such great works developed from them like the Book of Kells, the Book of Durrow, and the Book of Lindisfarne. Of the first two you can see them today at Trinity College in Dublin for there they are on public display. The detail is nothing short of incredible. For one book to be made would take a near life time to produce. However, since all the monasteries big and small were copying books this seemingly exhausting point is reduced on account of the number of books being created across the country. Lindisfarne for one example is stated that by the end of the 7th century had over 700 books. It is believed this was a typical average of all the monasteries. Ireland replaced Rome as the great library center of Europe.

Colum Cille

One of the giants of this new movement was Saint Colum Cille. He was born c. 540 AD into Celtic nobility and with him came natural respectability. By becoming a monk he alone elevated the movement even further, and added a lot of his family fortune to the monasteries as well. The Celtic Church started mimicking their Roman counterpart in terms of overall wealth. As much as they tried to stay humble and Colum Cille certainly lived this point by example, it was not to be:

wealth and opulence flourished. Colum Cille founded a monastery at Iona Scotland with just 12 close monastic friends and within 10 years the place grew to be an enormous institution in which had over a hundred satellite monasteries across Scotland and on the Amine land in Europe. Lindisfarne is an example of one of the satellite ministries of Iona.

Monastic Life and Principles

The Irish monastic order was nowhere near a strict as their Catholic mainland counterparts. In fact it was found that as late as the 12th century, sex and marriage amongst the monks were common practice. Though everyday living was hard, it was not further burdened by religious-based moral persecution. Monks went about their business in very friendly cooperative communal bases. Everyone was welcomed at no charge. However, it was mandatory to participate in the everyday activities of keeping the place in order and the community well fed. Archaeologist have uncovered that these monastic centres had everything they needed to survive, including gardens, livestock, and imported wines. They were Ireland's first mini cities. Up until now the only large, centrally populated areas in the country were the provincial fortresses like Cashel in Munster and Eman Macha in Ulster.

Everyday activities did involve a lot of prayer sessions. But seeing as the chapels were very small everything was on a rotational base. There were no general halls to speak of for eating so it is assumed meals were eaten at the monks little beehive homes. As evidence has shown the monks were well fed and had ample supply of both mead and wine. Livestock had to have been enormous for the copying of books was done on either sheep or cowhide vellum. The Book of Kells had over 400 pages to it when it was finished. When you consider each monastery had over 700 books in their libraries, that's a lot of animal hides. The highlight of the day's activities was book copying and reading. Not all the monks were writing but certainly all were reading what was being produced. The educational aspect of the community was one of the most exciting element of the monastic lifestyle. For the average Celtic Irishman being allowed to know the great mysteries, which up until now was restricted to the Druids, was simply unthinkable. Clearly this alone would have brought in converts to the new religion in droves.

Another really important aspect of the Celtic Christian society is their welcoming of women into their fold. As mentioned, this was often for reasons of marriage, but another reason, as Saint Brigitte will confirm, is many of the monasteries were run by abbesses. The Celtic mentally of equality between the sexes was carried on in the monastic order. Note the monasteries were not convents for women as became a later tradition once the Catholic Church was able to reassert its authority.

The Roman Catholic Church

The Roman Catholic Church still existed but had been seriously dwarfed due to the sweeping away of the Roman Empire in the west. The church you may say was a recluse so to speak, but was on the rebound. What slowed its growth was its concentration on the new royal courts. The Catholic Church was not open to the general public as the Celtic Christian church was. Their great books were reserved for the bishops and priests alone. As mentioned, only nobility and future priests were allowed a formal education if it was available at all. As such the Catholic Church grew very slowly by comparison.

Saint Augustine c. 520 AD had managed to start a Catholic diocese at Canterbury and from it a modest success in Sussex, Mercia, and East Anglia. However, he was in a land where the Saxons only tolerated the church for political reasons. What was becoming an irritant to the expansion was the new additional taxes the population was being subject to that did not exist in the Celtic Church system. At various times the Saxon,s annoyed with the whole ordeal, closed down the various regional churches and went back to their pagan beliefs. For the Catholics this was an added setback.

The Rise and fall of the Celtic Christian Church

Right from the get-go it has to be noted the Celtic Christian Church was not a centrally organized institution like the Roman Catholic Church. It was a series of independent monastic centre that covered all of Ireland and most of Scotland. The centres that were sending out missionaries were primarily Clonmacnose and Iona. Further it has to be remembered that everything was done in a very light and accommodating fashion, that even the Saxon peasants were finding pleasing to accept.

Circa 600 AD is more or less when the monks of the various monasteries started to migrate out. In Wales and Cornwall where there was already and Irish presence it was not hard to set up shop. There was of course a Welsh version of the Celtic Church started by Saint David in the region as well. Seeing the two were so similar in nature they could easily coexist. What distinguished the two was that the Irish monks were willing to move amongst the Saxons on the boarders of Wales and Cornwall, whereas the Welsh were content to stay with their own. The monastery of Iona, started by Saint Colum Cille, expanded into Northumbria principally by Saint Aiden.

On the main continent of Europe the Celtic Church expanded by Saint Columba (be aware this is a different person from Colum Cille) down the Rhine and to the very boarders of Italy. The farthest reach was Bobbio. About a dozen Celtic Monasteries had been set up and the Celtic Christian Church was fully established by 628 AD. What is remarkable is that the church carried on to expand east and west well into the 8th century where it was said that even the well-established Benedictine Church had been converted to Celtic Christian principles and were thus addressed as Irish Benedictine monasteries.

Saint Augustine, who was sent by Pope Gregory in 597 AD to Britain, came up against the stark reality that Britain was not a single nation. Each of the Saxon provinces was indeed separate kingdoms and you needed permission to cross the border. The Catholic Church was by 616 AD restricted to Sussex and Kent. The earlier gains that were made in East Anglia had been dramatically reduced to a quarter of their former size.

Where the Catholic Church was struggling just to exist, in Northumbria political events helped the Celtic Church to have a dramatic opportunity to expand with complete freedom. King Oswald came to the throne, and he had a very good ship with the ever pleasing Saint Aidan. As it was Saint Aidan was able to set up large new monasteries at Jarrow and Lindisfarne. From here like Colum Cille stretch the Celtic Church into the whole of Northumbria and across Mercia under King Penda.

Page from the Book of Kells illustration

By 663 AD the Celtic Christian Church had ¾ of Britain, Amorica, and had a solid grip on the central part of Europe. It was at this time the Roman Catholic Church felt it was time to confront the Celtic Church at the infamous Synod at Whitby up in Northumbria. A delegation had arrived from the various Celtic monasteries and the Roman Catholic Church sent a entourage headed by a brilliant speaker, James the Deacon, as he became to be known. The synod was presided over by King Oswy. Over the next few days representatives of both churches argued over what the main principles of the Christian faith should be. The James argued that the Roman Catholic Church was the descendant of Apostle Peter and just on this point alone the Celtic Church should be a follower of this institution. The Celtic monks argued back that god was not part of anyone's lineage, but each person was answerable to god individually; thus the Celtic Church had every right to exist separately and independently. It is said the Roman Catholic delegation offered other political benefits, which of course were kept secret from the debate, and as such King Oswy voted in favour of the Roman Catholic argument.

Over the next fifteen years there was a slow takeover of all the monasteries across Britain, by the Roman Catholic Church. As for Ireland it remained Celtic right up to when the Normans arrived in 1100s. On the continent you would think it would be easier still but it wasn't. One by one, however, the Celtic monasteries became Roman Catholic. It was said that not until the middle of the 13th century when the last Celtic Christian Church finally fall to the Roman Catholic rule. Perhaps it could be argued that the last Celtic influence both in political and cultural influence at last died out in this time period.

So now we know there were two Brennuses, where up to this point it was commonly believed there was only one. Though an unimaginably small point on a subject that for the most part barely gets a sentence in any conventional writing; it is important to note as no one could live for over a hundred years when the average age was only 40.

This is why I decided to take on this project in the first place; despite the volume of literature that has been written on the subject it all seems pretty much the same. The Celts first came into existence 800 BC, fought the Romans, lost, and suddenly we are now into Medieval Europe. Wow, how do you do that? How do you dismiss well over 1500 years of history like that? Obviously you must be callous, and it seems to me a lot authors are just that, sharing confusing or misleading points. So what? Who really cares? "I mean really," as Thomas Cromwell said to Richard Rich, "Our job is to administer for the least inconvenience for our sovereign." (statement during Henry VIII period to short cut the problem on getting rid of Anne Boleyn) And it seems that mentality has definitely reached well into the subject of the Celts.

As for Hannibal, who knows how many books have been written on him alone, but how many readers know that more than 60% of his armies were made up of the most ferocious warriors in all of Europe, the Celts. At the battle of Cannae virtually all of his centre ranks were Celts from Gaul. The cavalry on his right flank were 50% Gaul. And where ithe proof is ofof the heavy presence of the Celts in his ranks is that when they abandoned him in 212 BC, all Hannibal had left of his Carthaginians was a mere 1,500 men. Had it not been for the Celtic Confederacy, Hannibal would never have made it across Gaul, let alone Italy.

Iberia has definitely got to be one of the biggest secrets of Roman history. Most books I have read on this topic simply jump over it all together. Once the Second Punic War was over with Carthage we are now suddenly in Julius Caesar's time. That is unbelievable in itself. Over 150 years of Roman history simply disappears. Rome goes from being principally in Italy and Tunisia to now virtually the entire Mediterranean all in a snap of a finger. There are many mysteries surrounding Julius Caesar's campaign in Gaul and most of it centres on finance. Now when you include the Iberian War that had been draining the Roman reserves for years it is all very understandable. To many Roman senators Julius Caesar going into Gaul was deemed as another Iberia all over again;perhaps it maybe one war too many. Caesar's fast thinking after the Battle of Gergovia with Vercingeterix is what saved the Roman senate from putting a stop to his campaign all together. At this stage in the fighting the funding was at an all-time low. Iberia was the root cause of the Roman financial dilemma, something that should have been mentioned long ago but until now hasn't been.

And at last the Celts themselves. As we can now see a lot of writers portray them as simply being mindless, marauding nomads in much the same frame as the Vandals; we now know this isn't true in the slightest. Culturally speaking, the race has left so much to explore and so much today we enjoy because of them. I could mention their music but I am sure everyone around the world has at one point or another heard it. What I wanted to do in this book was point out their technology. I have traveled to numerous museums across Europe and the one thing I have found fascinating was the large presence of Celtic artifacts compared to Roman and Greek. The Copenhagen museum holds by far one of the best collection of Celtic art in the world. The number of swords, jewelry, armour, gold, tin pottery, and coinage there is overwhelming. These articats fill over a half a dozen rooms in the museum. By comparison Roman and Greek artifacts only make up three rooms together, primarily stone sculptures and coins. This I have found, except for in London, is the norm across the continent. The metallurgy skills of the Celts are such that their art has survived through the centuries far better than that of the superior cultures of the age. This is hardly something that should any longer be going unmentioned.

Of course the mentality and behaviour of the Celtic society is what many Pro-Roman historians gloat over as being their biggest downfall. Yet hopefully here I have been able to demonstrate that the legacy has actually been a centerpiece of our modern democracy. Celts were once, during the Hallstatt era, a centrally governed society, something we all recognized in much of Medieval Europe. However, something happened in the La Tène age and that was all dramatically removed; suddenly we now had a society where the political power was shared by the lower extremities of the hierarchy. We find that despite the Roman and later Saxon conquests of Britain alone, a Celtic democratic fury stayed with them. Britain was plagued by this subject for centuries; finally after Charles I's beheading, parliamentary democracy was there to stay. Clearly this is a Celtic phenomenon for in both Roman and Saxon heritage central, male rule was the prevailing pattern.

As we have seen now in this short little book, Ireland has a past that came unbelievably close to changing history as we know it. The chief reason it is not known to this point in time is of course the brutal suppression of it by 700 years of British rule. Let's face it, it's embarrassing to the British knowing that if Vortigern had of not called in the Saxons there may never have been an England as we know it today. Had the synod of Whitby not taken place Celtic Christianity would easily be today a major rival to the Roman Catholic Church. Why the Celtic Church was so popular was that it appealed to common, everyday folk. There was no church tax as was the case with the Roman institution. Who today would possibly believe this little green emerald island in the 5th century was as big a political threat to anything we know today?

Now do you see why I decided to write, "another book on the Celts?" There is still so much more to be discovered about these people than has been in the tens of thousands of books written thus far.

FURTHER READING

Ash, Geoffrey, *Kings and Queens of Early Britain,* Academy Chicago Publishing, Chicago,1990

Backhouse, Janet, *The Lindisfarne Gospels,* British Library Press, London, 1995

Bain, Ian, *Celtic Knotwork,* Constable Publishing, London 1986

Barnes, Dr. Ian, *The Historical Atlas of the Celtic World,* Chartwell Books, Inc. New York, 2010

Blair, John, *The Anglo-Saxon Age, A very short introduction,* Oxford University Press, London, 1984

Brown, Peter, *The Book of Kells,* Thames & Hudson , New York, 1980

Cahill, Thomas, *How the Irish Save Civilization,* Anchor Books, New York, 1995

Caesar, Julius, *The Conquest of Gaul,* Penguin Books, New York, 1982

Chadwick, Nora, *The Celts,* The Folio Society, London 2002

• *The Druids.* University of Wales, Wales, 1997

Cunliffe, Barry, *The Celts, A very short Introduction,* Oxford University Press, London, 2003

Davis, Courtney, *The Celtic Art Source Book,* Blandford Press, London 1988

Delaney, Frank, *The Celts,* Grafton Books, London, 1986

Dudley, D.R. and Webster G., *The Rebellion of Boudica,* Routledge, New York, 1962

Eluere, Christine, *The Celts: the First Masters of Europe,* Abrams, New York, 1993

Greene, Miranda (ed), *The Celtic World,* Rutledge, London, 1996

- *Dictionary of Celtic Myth and Legend,* Thames and Hudson, New York, 1997
- Green, M., *The Gods of the Celts,* Allan Sutton, Gloucester, 1968

Geoffrey of Monmouth, *History of the Kings of Britain,* Penguin, Hardmondsworth, 1925, 2000

Guest, Lady Charlotte (trans), *Mabigonion,* Ballantyne Press, London, 1910, 2000

Hamilton, Claire, *The Celtic Book of Seasonal Meditation,* Reed Wheel, York Beach, 2003

Kinsella, T., (trans), *The Táin,* Oxford University Press, Oxford, 1969

Konstan, Angus, *The Strongholds of the Picts,* Osprey Publishing Limited, London, 2010

Konstan, Angus, *British Forts in the Age of Arthur,* Osprey Publishing Limited, London 2008

Laing, Lloyd and Jenny, *The Picts and the Scots,* Allan Sutton Publishing Ltd, Gloucestershire Stroud, 1994

Lavin, P. *The Celtic World,* Hippocrene Books Inc. New York, 1999

Mathew, Caitlin, *The Celtic Tradition,* Elemental Book Limited, Rockport, 1995

MacAuley, Donald, (ed), *The Celtic Languages,* Cambridge University Press, Cambridge, 2008

Mackey, James, P., *An Introduction to Celtic Christianity,* T&T Clarkes, Ediburgh, 1995

Markale, Jean, *Women of the Celts,* Traditions Bear & Co. Rochester, 1989

- *King of the Celts,*   1996
- *The Holy Grail*   2001

Nennius, *British History and the Welsh Annals,* Philimore and Co., London, 1980

O'Hagain, Daithi, *Fionn Mac Cumhail,* Gill & MacMillian, Dublin, 1988

Piggett, S., *The Druids,* Thames and Hudson, London 1968

Pliny, (Jones W.H.S. –trans-), *Natural History VI,* Heineman, London, 1951

Radston, Ian, *Celtic Fortification,* The Tempus Publishing Ltd, Gloucestershire, 2006

Rankin, H.D., *Celts and the Classical World,* Croom Helm, London 1987

Shotter, david, *Roman Britain,* Rutledge, London, 2004

Stead, I.M., *Celtic Art,* British Museum, London, 1995

Tacitus, *The Annals,* Hacket Publishing Co. 2004

Tolkien, J.R.R., *On English and Welsh,* University of Wales Press, Cardiff, 1964

Wood, Juliette, *The Celts, Life, Myth and Art,* Duncan Baird Publishers Ltd, London, 2001

ACKNOWLEDGEMENT OF PICTURES

Tristan Logo, Ireland fun facts – Free sample
Celtic Empire Map, Maps of Celtic Europe, "get as word"
Map of Roman Briton, Sheppard Frere, Oxford University
Hotchdrof illustration, Graphica Press.
Green Celtic map, Emerson Kent, England, – Free sample
Celtic Warriors fighting, Trinity, Dublin
Tara Brooch, Vintage Ephemera, Bluespot.ca
Stonehenge, James knight, England
Monastery Scene, Amgueddfa Ilangollen museum
Illustration of Celtic Dwelling, wikispace.com
Illustration of Celtic wagon, wikispace.com
Ogham Lettering, Ancientscript.com
Book of Kells diagram, Art History Coloring Book, California